Let's Play and Learn Together

This book is playfully dedicated to our children and grandchildren whose laughter, hugs, and kisses are the best. What better way for us to discover how to make a baby giggle, how to join a toddler in song, and how to foster a child's gleeful interest in the world than through the wondrous times with our own families? We dedicate this book to our amazing children Jennifer, Rachel, Katie, Ryan, Kenneth, and Rachel, and to grandchildren Alex and Maya for teaching us that every belly kiss, puddle, silly song, ball, and bubble is an opportunity to connect and have fun. We love you to the moon and beyond!

First published in the USA in 2012 by
Fair Winds Press, a member of
Quayside Publishing Group
100 Cummings Center
Suite 406-L
Beverly, MA 01915-6101
www.fairwindspress.com

16 15 14 13 12   1 2 3 4 5

ISBN: 978-1-59233-495-7

Digital edition published in 2012
eISBN-13: 978-161058-178-3

Library of Congress Cataloging-in-Publication Data available

Cover and book design by Debbie Berne
Photography by Jade Albert
Additional photography:
    Shutterstock: pages 17, 63, 126, 131, 135,
    142, 145, 146, 151, 160, and 166
    Lisa Nalven Photography: pages 6, 10,
    and 159
    Tony Schreiber Photography page 94
Yoga mat courtesy: Kulae

Printed and bound in China

The information in this book is for educational purposes only. It is not intended to replace the advice of a physician or medical practitioner. Please see your health-care provider before beginning any new health program.

Let's Play and Learn Together

Fill Your Baby's Day with Creative Activities
That Are Fun and Enhance Development

RONI COHEN LEIDERMAN, Ph.D. and WENDY S. MASI, Ph.D.

contents

introduction

"Be him."

Alex had rummaged through his tattered cardboard box of figurines mixed with an assortment of blocks and crayons and held out one of his favorite plastic dinosaurs. His mother was happily reading the Sunday newspaper and drinking her morning coffee, content to relax as her son played nearby. Lowering the paper, Mom looked at her two-year-old son now surrounded by the entire contents of the box dumped on the floor.

"Be him, be him!" he repeated excitedly.

There was something about Alex's enthusiastic request that energized her as she put down her coffee, extended her hand to take the figurine, and kneeled down. Mom, in her very best dinosaur voice, and Alex, holding another rather ferocious-looking creature, began a dialogue about mountains, candy canes, and bugs. An outsider observing this scene may have seen a mother and son just playing a silly game. What this playful parent understood was that she had been invited into her son's wondrous world of play and imagination, where Alex was developing language, turn taking, and creativity and where a deep loving connection was being fostered.

Childhood is the time for play. It is the time for children to discover the world around them through exciting, novel, interesting, and meaningful experiences. From the first simple songs and books you introduce to your baby to the more complex games and activities you share with your preschooler, you are developing strong bonds and engaging in countless moments of closeness and glee with your child.

Play is much more than just fun and games. It is vital for cognitive, social, and emotional development because it helps children develop their dexterity, imaginations, and communication skills while promoting friendships, empathy, and conflict resolution. Through play, children practice and reinforce what they are learning. They experiment and figure out how to manage their emotions, practice adult roles, and conquer their fears. They process information and think through problems while tackling new information. As children experience successes, their self-esteem rockets and their love of learning soars.

There is no battery-operated, computer-generated, or cuddly toy that can take the place of a parent who understands, appreciates, and encourages play. Playful parents support their children as they acquire new skills and build their confidence through encouragement. When done mindfully, parent-child play is a beautiful dance. You tune in to your child's interests and rhythms, knowing when to structure the environment and join in the fun. You also realize when to move back and allow for undirected independent play. A playful parent understands child development and offers activities and games that are age-appropriate and set the stage for learning. Being patient, understanding, flexible, and fun are some of the keys for developing a wonderful relationship with your child. Having a sense of humor and not stressing over paint on the floor or sand in the shoes is a big plus!

As you read this book, you will find information about child development and the activities that are best suited for your children at different ages and stages. You will discover new ideas for songs and games that will delight and teach your child and ways that play can be incorporated into everyday moments like bathing, mealtime, and shopping. The toys we encourage are the most basic: blocks, balls, toy vehicles, pretend figures and props, books, and dolls for both girls and boys that provide the foundation for a well-stocked, playful home. Most important, we hope you will find that place inside yourself that is eager to sing, dance, run, jump, and play with your child in your very best dinosaur voice!

Playful parenting is an attitude and approach to raising children that makes life with babies, toddlers, and preschoolers easier, more delightful, and even more insightful. It is our hope that this book will help you enjoy and appreciate the value of play for learning and connecting with your child. Before you turn to the next page, take a moment to reflect on the experiences you treasure from your own childhood. Remember where you found your fun, joy, and bliss and bring that as a gift to your child. The rewards are priceless.

Play Ideas for Learning and Loving

Characteristics of a Playful Parent

Sings to, talks with, and reads to baby right from birth.

Describes what is happening throughout daily activities—"I am going to change your diaper now" and "What a big dog that is!"

Pays attention, tunes in, and responds to their child's attempts to communicate.

Talks with, not "at," their children to develop back-and-forth "conversations."

Uses language more often for communication than to give corrections, orders, and commands.

Is sensitive to the pacing of a "conversation" by giving ample time for children to respond and participate, even with early cooing, babbling, and simple words.

she will understand the meaning of words far before she can say them. Around twelve months old, babies begin to use "expressive jargon"— nonsense utterances that have the rhythm and intonations of the languages to which they are exposed.

Much to parents' delight, between twelve and eighteen months, most children develop a single-word vocabulary of between five and fifty words. They can point to pictures that you name and follow simple commands. By eighteen months, children begin putting words together and constructing their own unique short sentences, such as "all gone juice" and "want cookie." Toddlers constantly ask, "What's that?" and rapidly learn new words. They begin to use language in multiple ways: to greet people, ask for things, direct attention to something interesting, ask questions, describe, entertain, protest, and invite interaction. This is remarkable progress in an incredibly short time.

All children develop at their own pace. Some children move from single words and two-word combinations to conversations in a rapid burst while others gradually increase the length and complexity of their sentences. By the time most children are three years old, they are using at least three- or four-word sentences and are able to follow a two-part command. As they use longer sentences, they begin to master syntax; differentiate among past, present, and future; use adjectives, verbs, and pronouns appropriately; and differentiate singular and plural nouns. Often at this stage children overgeneralize a rule, for example, saying, "I eated all my cereal" or "I drinked up my milk."

Language is learned in the context of human interactions. Relationships are the portals for learning. A child who is raised in an environment rich with language, with many opportunities to express her wants and needs and participate in shared dialogues, has a significant advantage over a child raised in an environment where language exchanges are limited or confined to pronouncements and commands. Watching videos does not substitute for the experience of being listened to and talked with. Children need a loving adult to encourage and support their attempts to communicate.

for infants

Language activities during the first year of life are designed to "tune" babies in to the sounds and cadences of language, teach them the basic rules of conversation (I talk to you, then you talk to me), and help them develop a rudimentary understanding of language. Most important, these activities create awareness and a desire to communicate with the important people in their lives.

Talk to Me, Baby: Babies love to carry on conversations with interesting, and interested, adults. Research has shown that babies, regardless of their families' language or even their ability to hear, all have basically the same cooing and early babbling sounds. It is at about six months old that we see a drop of sound production in hearing-impaired babies and a difference in the sounds made by babies who are exposed to different languages.

Try imitating the sounds your baby makes to create a back-and-forth dialogue. Let your baby talk and then respond in kind. Vary your pace and pitch and see how long you can keep the conversation going. There may be times where your child needs a break in the action. Allow her to turn away and regroup. She will let you know when she's ready to play again.

» **Helps babies learn the basics of back-and-forth conversations**

What's Happening, Baby?: Often in the midst of all the busy things we need to do to care for our babies we forget to talk to them. Always let your baby know what's going to happen: "Now it's time to turn off the lights and go to sleep." "I'm going to pick you up and give you a big kiss!" "Here comes Daddy."

» **Sets the stage for your baby's understanding of language**

Ba Ba Ba Bumble Bee: Most babies babble the sound "da-da" before "ma-ma" because "d" is a hard consonant that is often part of a baby's vocal repertoire. At first, babies do not associate these sounds with their meanings, so mothers need not take it personally when they first hear only "da-da." "Ma-ma" comes a little later and is typically associated with distress, a meaningful and important communication reserved only for Mom.

Hard consonant sounds like ba ba and da da are often the first sounds that babies babble. Encourage your child to "talk" to you by imitating some of the sounds she makes. Get a "conversation" going with the following rhyme:

"Ba, ba, ba, bumble bee,
First I say ba to you,
Then you say ba to me,
Ba, ba, ba, ba, ba, ba, bumblebee."
» Tunes babies in to the sounds and cadences of language

A Picture Is Worth a Thousand Words: Place pictures or photographs within your baby's view near his changing table or tape them to the wall safely out of reach. Keep your child interested by changing the pictures every few weeks. Call his attention to the photos and talk to him about what he sees.
» Sets the stage for vocabulary development

Play with Mirrors »

Your baby will be more than a year old before she recognizes her own reflection in the mirror. Even so, she will have lots of fun watching herself from many different vantage points. Hold your baby up to a mirror and talk with her. Label body parts, touch the mirror, and let her look back and forth between you and your reflection. She will enjoy having an unbreakable mirror above or next to the changing table. If you have an unbreakable large mirror, lay your baby on top of it and see how she reacts to her image.

» Teaches babies to recognize them-selves and learn body parts

Get a Reaction with a Stone Face: See what happens when you are in the middle of an animated conversation with your baby and you stop and keep your face perfectly still. Observe your baby's efforts to get you smiling and talking again.

» **Demonstrates your baby's interest in engaging you in "conversation"**

Name That Toy: Children love to see, hold, taste, and manipulate objects. Give your baby toys to play with that can be easily named, such as a plastic cup, toy telephone, doll, spoon, stuffed kitten or dog, block, rattle, and pretend play food. Name each toy as he reaches for it. As he gets older, reverse the game and ask him to give you a specific toy.

» **Develops early vocabulary**

Read to Your Baby: A wise pediatrician we know used to give out a prescription for "reading a book a day" to all new parents. Making reading an important part of your family's daily routine fosters early literacy. Right from the start, your baby will enjoy being cuddled and read to. Babies like durable books with simple, brightly colored pictures or photographs.

» **Encourages a love of literature and fosters a loving connection with you**

for toddlers

During the toddler years, your child's understanding of language expands exponentially. His receptive vocabulary will be much larger than his expressive vocabulary, and he will show his understanding in multiple ways. Many of these language activities are designed to take advantage of this new stage and include following commands, participating in action songs, and expanding vocabulary.

Read to Your Toddler: As language is booming in the toddler months, reading becomes a favored and important activity. Toddlers request the same books over and over for months at a time because they love the familiarity that comes from repetition. When reading with your preschooler, pause and ask questions, such as "What do you think will happen next?" or "Why is the puppy sad?"
» Expands vocabulary and thinking skills while fostering a love of reading

Sing a Silly Song: Change the words of familiar children's songs to make them interesting and relevant to your toddler. Insert your child's name and give lots of opportunities for hugs and kisses to make it personal and fun. The more opportunities your child has to hear meaningful language, the faster he will tune in to your words.

Example: To the tune of "Frère Jacques":
Where is Susan, where is Susan?
Here she is, here she is.
Oh, I'm glad to see you, I'm so glad to see you,
Now let's hug. Now let's hug.
» Makes music fun and encourages language development

Tube Talk »

Talk to your baby through a cardboard tube and see how he reacts and responds to the change in your voice. Make all kinds of silly sounds.

» Facilitates auditory discrimination

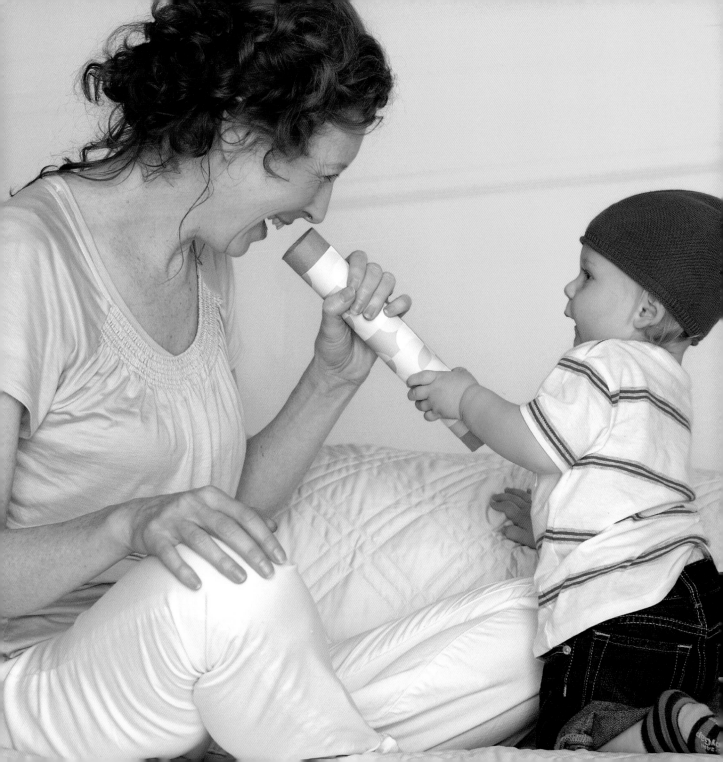

Turn an old clean sock into a new friend. Put a sock on your hand and move your fingers to make it talk. Use a variety of voices and hand motions to keep your child intrigued. And have another sock ready because your child will want one to play along, too.

» **Promotes conversational abilities**

My Very Own Library: Toddlers love books that are personal so make it all about her. Create your own library by filling a number of photo albums with words and pictures that capture the activities and important people in your child's life. Place one picture on each page and clearly label each one so that your photo album reads like a book. Here are examples of toddler albums:

"I can do it!": Find photos of your child and describe them with an "I can" sentence, such as "I can dance," "I can climb," or "I can hug Daddy."

"I love you!": Fill an album with people, pets, and things that are special to your child. Write an "I love . . ." message on the bottom of each page: "I love Mommy," "I love Daddy," or "I love cookies."

» **Encourages a positive sense of self and develops vocabulary reflective of your child's interests**

What Is It?: Find a special container for this game. Fill it with different everyday objects, such as spoons, play cars, miniature animals, or photos. Take turns reaching in and naming your chosen item. To make it harder, see whether your child can identify the item by feel.

» **Develops vocabulary and problem-solving skills**

Play Retrieval Games: Toddlers love following directions and showing you how much they can accomplish. It's all about "I can do it myself" now. Send your child on different errands. "Can you find your shoes?" "Please get me the ball." "Where's the cup?" Add silly directions like "put the sock on your head" to encourage a sense of humor.

» **Fosters the understanding of directions and encourages memory skills**

You've Got Mail: Make a mailbox by decorating an old shoe box or cardboard box and cutting a slit in the top. Give your child your junk mail and as she opens it, talk about the pictures, colors, and letters.

» **Develops an understanding of basic concepts**

for preschoolers

At this age, your child's language is becoming increasingly sophisticated and she is able to express more complex thoughts. Language activities are designed to increase vocabulary, expand syntax, and develop new concepts about the world. Talking with your child about anything and everything is the most important way you can encourage language development and expand your child's vocabulary. Everyday events like getting dressed, brushing teeth, cooking oatmeal, cleaning the table, and driving to school are opportunities for amazing conversations, questioning, and opinion seeking.

Stage a Treasure Hunt: Are you stuck inside on a rainy day? Make up a treasure hunt. Create picture clues by using photographs of objects in your home and gluing them to index cards. Each clue leads to the next clue until the special treasure is finally uncovered.

» Develops language and problem-solving skills

Fill in the Blanks: Sing familiar songs to your preschooler and leave out a word or a phrase. Young children love to demonstrate their knowledge, and through fun singing games, they are learning about language and turn taking.

» Expands vocabulary and memory

Be a Card-Carrying Family: Don't throw out those holiday cards that come with family photos. Preschoolers enjoy pointing out and naming friends and relatives for months to come.

» Deepens emotional connections and fosters social skills and memory

A Big Box of Words »

Your preschooler is learning the power of words and becoming interested in interpreting the marks on a page. Let her decorate a special word box and gradually fill it with index cards that have the words she is interested in learning to "read."

Start with things that are important to your child, such as her name. Write it in clear, bold print on one side and paste a picture of her on the back of the card. Add favorite relatives, pets, friends, toys, and objects. Take out one or two cards at a time and see whether she can guess whose picture is on the back by recognizing the symbol of a name. Be sure to let her have a turn asking you if you can "read" the card.

» Introduces beginning reading skills

Time for Puppet Talk: Puppets are a wonderful way to initiate conversations and encourage the expression of feelings. This is a time to have fun and be silly. Let your puppet say all kinds of outrageous things and see how your child's puppet responds. Use the puppets to "talk" about feelings and fears.

» **Encourages back-and-forth conversations and vocabulary skills**

Guessing Games: Hide a small toy or object behind your back, give your child clues, and see whether she can guess what you are holding. "I'm holding an animal that says 'moo'" or "I have something that we use for eating ice cream."

» **Promotes vocabulary development and thinking skills**

Create Your Own Silly Book: Make your own silly flip book by cutting pictures out of magazines and gluing them onto construction paper. Punch holes in the sides of the pages and string them together loosely with yarn. Cut all the pages into thirds so that you can create silly mix-ups as you flip the pages.

» **Facilitates interest in reading**

Make Food for Thought: When your child is ready for school, pack a "napkin note" with her lunch. Her teacher will be delighted to read it aloud and your child will enjoy hearing from you in the middle of the day.

» **Highlights the importance of written communications**

Send Me a Letter: It's fun for preschoolers to receive mail. Surprise your child by sending him a real letter. Include interesting stickers or photos. Print your message in simple bold text. He will soon try to "read" his letter on his own.

» **Develops an interest in reading**

strong and healthy
Developing Motor Skills, Strength, and Agility

Ways to Facilitate Motor Skills Development

Give your child space to move and explore in a safe environment, but limit the time your child is kept in restricted spaces like cribs or playpens.

Encourage and support, but avoid teasing. It can be tempting to keep moving a toy slightly out of reach to keep your baby moving, but be careful not to frustrate your child.

During playtime, place your baby on a variety of surfaces, sometimes on his stomach and other times on his back. Try a soft, textured surface like a carpet and a clean smooth surface like a play mat. Avoid hard surfaces, such as tile, where your baby could get hurt.

Be careful not to overuse baby equipment like swings, walkers, and strollers. As much as possible, let your baby move freely.

During the first three years of life, your child will learn to sit, crawl, stand, walk, run, jump, climb, throw, catch, push, pull, carry, walk up and down stairs, and perhaps even pedal a tricycle. He will also learn to use a fork and spoon, hold a crayon, and button his shirt. All these skills take coordination, strength, balance, and practice.

All children have their own developmental timetable for the acquisition of motor skills and they will master both gross and fine motor skills at their own pace. Crawling, walking, jumping, and climbing involve large muscles. Reaching, grasping, cutting, and drawing involve eye-hand coordination and small muscles. Right from the beginning you can help your child enjoy moving and develop flexibility, confidence, and perseverance. A love of physical activity comes naturally to most children, making it easy to engage their interest. Providing opportunities for your child to develop and experiment with newly developed skills and take on new challenges with gusto sets the stage for a healthy active life.

Newborns have relatively little control over their bodies and their movements. Their heads are large in comparison to their bodies, and their neck muscles are weak. They often startle when they hear loud sounds, responding with their entire bodies. By three or four months, babies begin to reach and grasp, bat at dangling toys, grasp small objects and bring them to their mouths, and kick their legs. Soon they begin to turn from side to side, and between four and eight months they slowly master sitting.

Within seven to eleven months, most babies start crawling and learn to coordinate the movements of their arms and legs. They now use their developing motor skills to achieve desired goals. They will figure out how to get to the toy they want, pick up a tiny piece of lint from the carpet to see how it tastes, and pull themselves to a stand to look over the bars of the crib. Learning to pull to a stand and learning to get back down don't happen at the same time. At this stage, you may discover your baby standing up in his crib, crying, unable to get himself down.

Babies learn to get around in different ways. Some propel themselves on their stomachs in an army crawl, some get up on all fours and creep, and others hitch forward on their bottoms. Although it's not typical, some babies may never crawl, instead moving directly from sitting to standing and walking.

Some children burst into walking, while for others, the process is more laborious. Children who are on the heavier side, have low muscle tone, are temperamentally cautious, or focus their energies on other developmental tasks like talking may be slower to walk. The normal limits for walking are broad and extend from eight to twenty months.

Walking quite literally brings a new worldview. Growing a foot taller makes the world look different and getting around is different, too. Turning, sitting down, and going under and over are all different from this new perspective. For parents, walking brings new challenges. All of a sudden many things are in your child's reach that were previously safely out of the way and new dangers abound. Babyproofing your home starts at birth, yet once your child starts walking it takes on greater meaning and significance.

Between the age of one and two children learn to forcefully swing their arms and direct this motion in a particular direction. In other words, they learn to throw and pound, and although not particularly accurate, they delight in this newfound power. They also become intrigued with carrying things and will try to push, pull, and carry as large an object as possible.

Toddlers also become increasingly adept at climbing. Stairs are often the first challenge, but nothing is sacred. Furniture, beds, cabinets, and coffee tables are all seen by the toddler as obstacles to be explored and conquered. Of course, getting down is not as easy as getting up. This is the age where constant parental supervision is required to keep your child safe. Even heavy stable furniture can topple over when a child uses open drawers as stairs.

Children are also refining their fine motor skills and becoming interested in stacking blocks, turning the pages of a book, or transferring small objects into containers. This is the age where they begin to enjoy

Characteristics of Playful Parents

Has realistic expectations; most motor skills can't be rushed

Encourages but doesn't frustrate children with activities that are too challenging

Respects children's individual temperament

Creates a healthy lifestyle with quality food and exercise right from the start

Spends time outdoors to give children an opportunity to be around nature and experience a variety of new, interesting places in which they can crawl, run, and jump

Makes physical activity part of the daily family routine. (Takes family walks, play ball, swim, or walk the dog together)

pegboards, simple puzzles, and pounding benches or trying to put your keys into the door lock.

Preschoolers have mastered walking and climbing and now are ready to run, jump, slide, catch, and throw. They are beginning to hop, balance on one foot, and climb up and down stairs like adults. At this age, children enjoy riding tricycles and pulling wagons. They thrive on exercise as long as it's on their own terms. Physical games are fun as long as the rules are loose and flexible.

Children now become interested in tearing, cutting, pasting, and drawing. Preschoolers are adept at using art and craft materials like crayons, markers, glue, and glitter. Most three-year-olds can draw a circle and a cross. They are beginning to draw people, although their attempts are relatively crude and lacking in detail. Provide lots of paper and art materials and don't be surprised when there are scribbles on your table or the wall, as children may have challenges with boundries and self-control.

Your child's self-help skills are also improving. He can now pour his own juice, put on his shoes, and with help get on most of his clothes. What used to take five minutes now requires patience and encouragement because he wants to do everything himself.

for infants

Babies will naturally develop physical strength, flexibility, and mobility if they are provided with the opportunity to move freely. Although there is little we can do to speed the developmental timetable, these activities will provide your child with the opportunities he needs to grow and develop.

→ **Play Beach Ball Bingo**
Fosters motor control and balance

Play Beach Ball Bingo: Put your baby on a slightly deflated beach ball or thickly rolled towel. For young babies, put them on their tummies and gently rock the ball back and forth. For sturdier older babies, have them sit supported on the beach ball to encourage muscle strength and balance.

» **Fosters motor control and balance**

Kick, Kick, Kick, and Kick Some More: To encourage your baby to strengthen his leg muscles, change his position so that instead of batting at his hanging toys with his hands, he can kick them with his feet. Not only will this develop his motor skills, but it will also give him an interesting new challenge.

» **Develops strength and coordination**

See the World from Different Perspectives: Hold your baby high on your shoulders to let him view novel sights and use muscles to maintain his posture and keep his head up. Change your baby's position throughout the day to strengthen muscle groups and encourage different motions. When your baby has head control, place him in a sitting position on your lap or safely support him with large pillows for as long as he is comfortable and happy. Offer toys to your baby, encouraging him to move and regain balance.

» **Encourages muscle tone and development**

« Fly Me to the Moon

Babies enjoy motion and the feeling of being suspended in the air. Hold your baby on her stomach with your hands fully supporting her. Gently move up and down and back and forth with sound effects as she takes off into space.

» **Gives opportunity for body movement and stimulation**

Make Some Tummy Time: Your baby must always be put to sleep on her back for safety reasons. Because children spend so many hours sleeping in that position, it is vital to give your child opportunities to be on her stomach when she is awake. While she is on her tummy, give her interesting toys like balls with chimes that make sounds with a simple touch. Most important, get down on the floor and give her the best toy of all to interact with—you! Note that some babies are uncomfortable on their stomachs, so watch for signals that she has had enough tummy time and change her position.

» **Strengthens head, neck, and chest muscles—It is also a precursor to crawling**

Practice Baby Sit-Ups: If your baby has good head control, hold him under his arms while he is lying on his back and gently guide him to a sitting position. As your child gains muscle tone and strength, do these sit-ups by holding his hands and slowly bringing him to sit. You will soon see him develop strength and balance and begin to pull himself up faster than you are guiding him.

» **Develops motor skills and head control**

Play That Funky Music: Babies love to stand with support, so much so that sometimes it's hard to get them to bend their legs and sit down! Support your baby under his arms (never hold babies by their hands because you can dislocate their shoulders) while he's standing. Sing a song and watch him bop to the music.

» **Develops a love of music and movement**

for toddlers

Toddlers are notorious for always being on the move. Once they develop the abilities to walk, run, and climb they are in constant motion. These activities take advantage of children's natural desires to test their limits and learn new skills.

Organize an Obstacle Course: Set up an obstacle course using cloth tunnels, sofa cushions, cardboard boxes, and toddler slides. Your child will love to crawl, climb, stand, and walk through, around, over, and under all the obstacles you create. Describe her actions as she takes the challenge. She will be developing motor skills and gaining an understanding of spatial concepts at the same time.

» **Reinforces spatial concepts—over, under, around, through and develops agility and coordination**

Take Those First Sticky Steps: Cut a piece of clear contact paper at least 2 feet (61 cm) long. Remove the backing and tape the contact paper, sticky side up, to the floor or carpeting. Toddlers will have fun running, jumping, dancing, or just standing on the paper while wiggling their toes on the sticky surface.

» **Develops sensory awareness and muscle strength**

Let's Push: After your child has started walking, a pushcart or push-along corn popper can help him practice. Pushcarts are sometimes designed as shopping carts, trucks, baby carriages, vacuum cleaners, or lawn mowers, which make them not only useful to the early walker but also fun for pretending.

» **Introduces new motor skills and encourages pretend play**

Get a Perfect "10" on the Balance Beam: A makeshift balance beam can help your toddler improve her balance and coordination. At first, put a 6-foot (1.8 m) length of board, about 4 to 6 inches (10 to 15 cm) wide, directly on the floor. As your child's balance improves, you can start to raise the beam a little by putting several books under each end.

» **Encourages a sense of balance**

Pull Some Strings: Once your child has mastered walking, he will enjoy pulling something along behind him. There are many types of pull toys that make interesting noises to keep the fun going. You can make your own by tying his favorite toys together with short pieces of string or ribbon.

» **Develops motor control and coordination**

Stack 'Em Up: Toys that fit together let your toddler practice new manipulative skills. Stacking and nesting cups, which also can be used to build towers, are classics. Six or eight plastic cups of the same size work especially well for the early "nester" because they can fit together in any order.

» **Provides opportunities for fine motor skill development**

Have a Ball: Though your child probably can't catch yet, that doesn't mean you should ignore the play possibilities of balls. Given a large rubber or inflatable ball, your toddler can kick it, roll it, and stop it with his hands and feet when you roll it back.

» **Encourages basic running, catching, and kicking skills**

→ **Organize an Obstacle Course**
Reinforces spatial concepts—over, under, around, through—and develops agility and coordination

« Build Large Block Towers

Toddlers especially like large blocks that allow them a feeling of power as they build towers as large as themselves. Large cardboard bricks do the trick. You can purchase them or construct lightweight blocks by filling old diaper boxes with newspaper and taping them shut.

» **Develops fine and gross motor skills**

All Aboard!: Create a "train" by having your toddler sit on a towel or blanket and gently pull her around the room. This activity challenges her balance. First stop can be a visit to the "zoo," next stop wherever your imaginations take you.

» **Fosters both balance and pretend skills**

Rip It to Shreds: Your old magazines are the perfect "toy" to keep your toddler occupied and help him develop those important fine motor skills. Show him how to tear, shred, and crumple the pages while you talk with him about the pictures. You can end with a collage or a game of garbage-can basketball.

» **Gives opportunities to develop finger and hand strength and control**

for preschoolers

Preschoolers are ready for new motor challenges. These activities introduce children to some of the basic skills they will need to participate in physical games and activities while providing fun interactive ways to develop and practice new abilities. Physical fitness is the perfect way for families to play together and for children to begin to play simple games with friends.

Toss the Beanbag: Beanbags are just the right weight and size for little hands to throw. Try tossing them into a basket or box. Make a line with tape on the floor and have your child stand on the line to see if she can make a basket. Move the line farther as she masters the game. Beanbags are also ideal for learning how to catch, so let the fun begin!
» **Develops basic throwing and catching skills**

Kick Up a Storm: Give your child a large, soft ball and show him how to kick it along in front of himself. Add to the fun by having a "goal" that you and your child can alternately kick the ball into.
» **Teaches turn taking and an understanding of rules and encourages sportsmanship**

Freeze Frame: Play all sorts of music from classical to rock. When you stop the song, everyone has to freeze until the music starts again. Children enjoy the "contest", but remember that this isn't about winning or losing. Everyone is a winner in the game.
» **Develops attention skills and motor control and teaches how to play games with rules**

Score a Home Run: See how far your child can hit the ball using a light plastic bat and a Wiffle ball placed on a T. This activity takes time and practice and nothing is more reinforcing of efforts than the powerful feeling your child will have when she whacks the ball.

» **Encourages muscle strength and agility**

Hide-and-Seek, Don't Peek: There's a reason why children all over the world and for generations have played hide-and-seek. Let your child decide how long the counter will have his or her eyes closed before looking for the hider. It may be easy to find your preschooler because he will probably be giggling as you search for him. This is so much fun that children never seem to tire of the game.

» **Encourages social and problem-solving skills and spatial awareness**

Stuffed Liked Sardines: Hide-and-seek reaches a new level when you change the rules to play with a group of children and adults. One person hides and everyone else searches. Once you find the hider, you hide with her until everyone squeezes together into the "sardine can."

» **Fosters problem-solving skills while encouraging social interactions**

Jump to It: This is a variation on a time-tested universal game. Using chalk outside or masking tape inside, create a series of squares that your child can jump into and from square to square. In time, introduce hopping by holding your child's hands. Before you know it, he'll be jumping and hopping on his own.

» **Develops agility and balance**

What Can You Do Next?: Write out some new challenges for your child on small pieces of paper, such as standing on one foot, jumping three times, touching toes, turning around four times, and other fun challenges. Put the papers in a small basket or paper bag. Let your child close her eyes and choose a challenge. Read it to her and see if she can follow the directions. Add more complicated challenges, such as hopping, or combine a few of them for more challenging fun. Remember to take a turn yourself because preschoolers enjoy being in charge and giving directions.

» **Develops an array of motor skills and encourages attention and direction following**

Have Some Flashlight Fun: Get your child moving by having him chase the light from a flashlight. The most fun comes when he is the flashlight director and you do the chasing.

» **Fosters a joy of movement**

Crack, Bubble, Pop! »

Tape a strip of clear contact paper onto the floor, sticky side up. Stick a path of bubble-wrap packing material onto the contact paper. Encourage your child to walk barefoot on the path, jumping and popping the bubbles along the way.

» **Encourages strength and agility**

all about me
Developing a Positive Self-Image

All children are unique right from birth. They have their own genetic makeup and combined with their inborn temperament and your special way of interacting with them, develop a personality that begins to quickly emerge. Some children are easygoing and calm down quickly. Others are fussier and require swaddling and rocking to stop crying. Some babies nurse for long periods of time, content to be in their mothers' arms. Other babies are less cuddly. When you respect your child's unique way of dealing with the world, she comes to understand that she is important and valued. The care you generously give to your baby sets the stage, moment by moment, for the building of her self-identity and feelings of self-worth. The emotional "piggy bank" that you invest in now with love and attention for your baby will yield valuable results for her in the years ahead and most likely into her adulthood.

Newborns seem to have two simple emotions: distress and contentment, which are expressed by either crying or not crying. In actuality, there is much more happening. They are taking in their brand-new environment through observation and sensory input. With an inborn need and desire to be held and touched, your baby is developing a sense of identity, and soon her emotional repertoire will expand to include joy, sadness, surprise, curiosity, and love.

Self-awareness unfolds as a developmental process beginning at birth. Babies spend a lot of time discovering their own bodies in the first few months. They suck their fingers, grab their toes, and gaze at their hands. As the weeks and months progress, they begin to initiate social interactions with their first smiles, laughs, and cooing, demonstrating the beginning of the development of a sense of self. Soon they pay attention to their own name, express a variety of emotions, show a preference for certain people and toys, and imitate their parents' actions.

During baby's first year, the parents' task is to ensure that their child develops a sense of trust of the environment, his caretakers, and himself. That is why it is so vitally important to respond consistently and lovingly to babies' cries and needs. You cannot spoil a young baby

Ways to Facilitate a Positive Self-Image

Respond lovingly and consistently to your child.

Understand and respect your child's unique personality and temperament.

Model genuine care for others.

Express love for your child through what you say and do.

Demonstrate encouragement for your child's efforts.

Use positive discipline while understanding that discipline means teaching, not punishing.

by holding, cuddling, rocking, and nurturing too much. Babies whose needs are attended to by consistent loving adults will actually cry less often and be calmed more quickly than babies who are left on their own to "cry it out." By responding to your baby's needs, you are teaching her that she is important, that she has an effect on the people in her world, and that she is valuable and worthy of the love and devotion of the most important people in her world: her parents.

There may come a period when your toddler finds it upsetting to be without you. Because you are so vitally important to him and responsible for making him feel happy and secure, separation anxiety occurs when you leave, even for short periods of time. Because all children have their own unique temperament, some children may be happy to wave bye-bye when Mommy goes to work. Other children may suddenly feel frightened and upset when Daddy merely leaves the room for a few moments. Respect your child's personality and guide him gently with reassurance and consistency until he is able to move past this challenging time.

By around eighteen months old, a toddler will look into his reflection in a mirror and actually understand that the image is, in fact, him. He now has self-identity. This is an important time, for toddlers are developing not only self-recognition but also self-confidence. They can express themselves, think about themselves and their actions, and realize that they have an effect on others.

Another milestone that shows a sense of self-identity is your child's strong independence. Wanting to do everything by herself, whether or not she can actually do it, is part of the normal developmental process. This is the time when meals become a bit of a struggle, with your two-year-old knowing exactly where she wants to sit, what she wants to eat, which bowl and spoon she wants to use, and how she wants to feed herself. This surge of identity is also the time when the dreaded "no!" gets expressed loudly and often. Children now realize they have choices, and their decisions may not jibe with yours. They know what they are allowed to do and what is prohibited, and they want to test limits. Children at this stage are exerting authority and declaring to the world, "I know who I am and what I want!"

This time can be frustrating for parents. Their typically compliant baby now has a mind of his own. Through understanding the normalcy of your child's newly forming independence comes a remarkable time of discovery for both of you. Yes, it may be more difficult to get your child dressed, bathed, and fed, taking the time to acknowledge that today he wants his toast cut into triangles and served on the yellow plate. Putting a puzzle together may be more frustrating now because he wants to do it all by himself, and it may be a struggle in the bath if he doesn't want his hair washed. But these times are indicative of a huge developmental accomplishment of self-assertion and self-assurance.

Your child always watches you closely and uses you as a model to teach her about the consequences of her actions and the choices she makes. She is expressive of her emotions and demonstrates them grandly, whether they are anger, joy, shame, or pride.

Empathy, understanding how other people feel, is a learned behavior that your child develops by watching how you interact with her and others. Always remember that you are your child's first and most important teacher.

Characteristics of a Playful Parent

Understands and respects their child's developmental timetable

Appreciates the importance of developing a sense of trust and independence in their child

Models confidence, nurturance, and patience

Is mindful of their own emotions

Responds to baby's needs lovingly and consistently

Helps their child be a good problem solver and build self-confidence

Labels their own and their child's emotions

Gives their children support in learning new skills without doing it for them

for infants

Activities for infants are designed to help them become aware of their own bodies. They will come to understand that they have arms, hands, legs, feet, and even a belly button. They are beginning to realize that they are a person, separate and apart from their parents. At the same time, these activities are designed to develop a positive sense of self: "I am a baby who is special, loved, and cared for."

Connect Harmoniously: Music is the universal way to connect with others. Play your favorite songs and expose your child to a variety of beautiful music while you dance and sing. You don't have to know the words, singing just "la la la" and swaying to the beat are perfect.
» Fosters listening skills and joint connection

Make Baby Laugh: Babies love to laugh at silly words. See what funny-sounding words or phrases conjure up belly laughs for your child. The famous, "I'm going to get you" with accompanying tickles or hugs is a sure way to get things going.
» Encourages a sense of humor

Massage: Babies thrive on loving touch. A soothing massage each evening before bedtime is a wonderful way to express your love and encourage your baby's awareness of her body.
» Develops body awareness and a positive relationship

Peak-a-Boo Games »

When things go out of sight, babies think they no longer exist. That's why games like peek-a-boo are so special. It shows your child that even though she can't see Mommy and Daddy for a few moments, they are still there. Another way to help them learn is by calling to them from another room. Saying, "I'm coming, Maya! Here comes Daddy," will help your baby begin to comprehend that you exist even when she can't see you.

» Develops social awareness and object permanence and promotes a sense of security

for toddlers

Toddlers are beginning to express a more complex range of emotions and becoming interested in learning about themselves and others. These activities will give parents and their toddlers playful opportunities to expand their worldview.

Look-in-the-Mirror Game: Put a red dot of lipstick on your toddler and distract her for a few moments before putting her in front of a mirror. If your child reacts to her image by touching her nose, indicating that she realizes that there is something odd about what she is seeing, it shows she understands that she is seeing her own face. Most babies between fifteen and twenty-four months will touch their faces because they have a picture in their minds of what they usually look like.
» **Promotes self-awareness and identity**

Body Tracing: This is a fun way to help your child learn body parts, develop self-awareness, and expand his language. Have him lie down on a large piece of paper and trace the outline of his body. Together you can fill in the eyes, nose, and mouth and add hair and accessories.
» **Advances a sense of self**

Picture This!: Keep a stack of up-to-date photographs of people and pets who are special to your child. Unlike a photo album, loose pictures invite storytelling because you can lay out many pictures at the same time. Your child will enjoy looking through the images and talking about her favorite people. Another variation is to glue pictures on jar lids. Your toddler will enjoy putting the lids in and out of a coffee can and at the same time you can talk about the photos. You can also affix magnet tape to the backs of photos of favorite objects and people and put them on a magnetized cookie sheet. Talk about the pictures and once your child has become familiar with them, prompt him with questions like, "Where is your cuddly bear?" "What should we eat for lunch?" or "Where is Suzy?"

» **Encourages social awareness and language skills**

Teach Me to Care: Playing with baby dolls teaches toddlers how to express love, care for others, and show empathy. These traits are valuable for all people, so don't be hesitant to let both your son and your daughter play with dolls. Help your child give his baby doll a bath. This is also a great way to reinforce body awareness: "Let's wash his hair," "Make sure we don't get soap in his eyes," "Don't forget to put soap on his toes."

» **Develops empathy and a sense of self**

Can We Talk?: At the end of each day, include a review as part of your bedtime routine. By discussing the day's activities, you and your child will have the opportunity to revisit the interesting, fun, happy, and special moments you shared.

» **Supports language development, memory skills, and social awareness**

→**Teach Me to Care**
Develops empathy and a sense of self

How Do You Feel?: As children mature, they become more adept at talking about their feelings and become more appropriately in control of their emotions. When you label how your child seems to be feeling, you validate her feelings and give her words that she will begin to use to describe her emotions. "You are so mad!" or "That made you so happy!" invites word usage and a sense that you understand how your child is feeling.

» Encourages emotional awareness and language development

Me and My Shadow: Children are fascinated with light and movement. Shine a flashlight in a darkened room where you toddler can jump on the moving light. When outside on a sunny day, be sure to take notice of you and your child's shadows. When you are on a walk with your child, talk about her shadow: sometimes it will be big, sometimes it will be small. Can you run and jump on your shadow? What happens to your shadow when you wiggle your fingers?

» Reinforces body awareness and supports language development

Follow the Leader: For a fun way to play follow the leader, imitate the sounds and gestures that your child makes. She will love being in charge and directing you to do what she does. Label things as you go: "I'm following you up the stairs." "I'm jumping with you." "You are running fast."

» Develops a sense of accomplishment and language skills while fostering coordination

Hand-Washing Challenge »

If you want your little one to get in the habit of washing his hands, make it fun by placing a small basin filled with soapy water next to the sink. Hide a toy in the bottom for him to find as he completes the activity. Change the water and toy regularly throughout the day and always supervise water play.

» Encourages independence

for preschoolers

Now is the time to help your child understand his emotions, interpret the feelings of others, and develop self-control. These activities are designed to deepen your child's understanding of himself and others.

What Makes You Happy?: At this age, children love to discuss the things that make them happy, sad, or frightened. Also talk about things that make Mommy and Daddy feel those ways. Not only does asking them about their feelings help them recognize emotions, but it also gives them an understanding of the things that make others feel the same way.

» Develops a sense of self and emotional awareness

I Love You More: A playful and endearing word game is to fill in the blank to the statement, "I love you more than ___." For example: "I love you more than the highest building!" "I love you bigger than Uncle Ryan!" "I love you deeper than the ocean!" Take turns filling in the blanks and making up interesting sentences to complete.

» Encourages emotional development and language skills

I Did It!: Take photos of special accomplishments and put the pictures in a photo album that your child can look at and show others. Pictures can be of anything that she did that she is proud of, such as riding a bike, building a tall block tower, swimming across the pool, brushing her own teeth, or sharing a favorite toy with her sister.

» Fosters self-identity and positive self-image

Thumbs Up! Thumbs Down!: Fold a big piece of construction paper in half and ask your child to draw or paste magazine pictures of things he likes on one side of the paper and things he doesn't like on the other side. It's a fun way to engage in conversation and to let your child know it is okay to have strong feelings about things.

» Develops thinking skills and self-understanding

Take It Step by Step: One of the best ways to teach your child or to encourage her to do something she may be fearful of is through stories. Pick something that you are working on, such as sleeping in her new bed, going to school for the first time, or learning how to swim. The storybook can describe the activity step by step to completion. Preschoolers love these stories and learn great lessons while reading with you.

» Encourages independence and a positive self-image

→**Thumbs Up! Thumbs Down!**
Develops thinking skills and
self-understanding

let's pretend
Developing a Child's Imitation and Imagination Skills

The two simple words "let's pretend!" are perhaps the best representation of the magic of early childhood. After all, who else but a young child can fly a rocket ship to Mars, share afternoon tea with a favorite stuffed animal, or vanquish monsters from under his bed? Not only does pretend play offer hours of fun but also the opportunities for children to develop cognitively, socially, and emotionally are endless.

Pretend play is one of the important hallmarks of early childhood. Children spend hours creating their own worlds, developing their own games, and playing out their own unique fantasies. But pretend play is more than just a way for children to pass time; it's one of the key ways that children learn to make friends, deal with difficult emotions, sort through complex problems, and develop their creative abilities.

Pretending begins with simple imitation—children mimic what they see others do and in the process learn important skills. Gradually, as children become more capable of representational thought and are exposed to a variety of experiences and ideas, they develop their own repertoire of play ideas. As their play becomes more advanced, they begin to see things from the perspective of others and understand that other people have thoughts, feelings, and emotions. When they begin pretending with peers, they learn how to communicate effectively and develop problem-solving and negotiation skills.

During the first year of life, young children learn to imitate simple actions. Stick your tongue out at a young baby and she is likely to return the gesture. Around six months of age, new skills develop. She will bang, clap, and wave bye-bye in response to your actions and watch you carefully as you manipulate her toys so she can learn how to gain control over her world.

Toddlers become quite adept at imitating your actions. They will jabber into a toy telephone, try to put keys in a lock, and sweep the floor with a broom, copying the important things they have seen you do. It's difficult to tell exactly when pretend play begins because we can't be sure whether toddlers are imitating something they've seen us

Ways to Facilitate Pretend Play

Provide your child with a variety of props and keep them organized in a way that your child can easily access them on his own.

Follow your child's interests. For example, when your child becomes intrigued by animals, create a veterinarian's office in your living room.

Join in the fun. Act out your "assigned" characters with gusto.

do or actually pretending to be engaged in the activity. If your little one puts a spoon in his toy duck's mouth, for example, is he simply using a spoon the way he knows it's meant to be used or is he pretending to feed the duck?

Typically, pretend play is thought to begin around eighteen months of age. Developmental psychologist Jean Piaget believed we could tell when a child is pretending by his "coy smile." Early pretend play most often centers on familiar activities. Young children play house, store, restaurant, or doctor. They pretend to bathe a doll, drive a car, talk on the telephone, or put a stuffed animal to bed.

As children approach the two-year mark, subtle changes occur in their style of playing. Play episodes become more complex, props become increasingly varied, and all kinds of nuances are added to their stories. As children enter the preschool years, their themes become more elaborate and fantasy based. They might fly spaceships, sail with pirates, become princesses, or slay giants. This is also the stage when children typically begin to take on the roles of characters they create and to participate in pretend play with peers. For young preschool children, parents are still their preferred partners. Additionally, children's pretending is more advanced when they play with parents or older children.

Pretend play gives young children the opportunity to be in control. They can do what they're interested in; make choices about what they're going to do, who's going to be what, and what's going to be what; and decide how the story's going to unfold. With pretend play, children can work through difficult emotions safely. Playing mommy and baby can help a child come to terms with the arrival of a new sibling. Playing teacher can make her more comfortable starting preschool. Playing hospital can alleviate her fear of doctors. Playing superhero can help her gain control over her fear of monsters.

Pretending is greatly facilitated by the kinds of materials we provide. The right types of props are important, but they don't need to be elaborate or numerous. Early pretending is often facilitated by toys that look somewhat realistic. A very young child, for example, is more likely to talk on a toy telephone than to pretend a banana is a phone. As they get older, they'll take any object and turn it into a telephone, but early on, children have trouble overriding the functions that something is supposed to have in order to have it do something else. Kitchen sets, doctor kits, toy tools, grocery-related props, and other toys with familiar life themes are ideal for early imaginative play. Dolls, toy animals, and small vehicles also are useful, especially because they can fit into so many stories and settings. Miniature plays sets, blocks, cars, and plastic farm animals encourage children to build their own worlds and direct the action.

Characteristics of a Playful Parent

Engages in play but doesn't take over

Allows their child to be in control—for example, if the "restaurant" serves ice cream with ketchup and mustard, Mom and Dad still enjoy their meal

Helps extend the play by providing new ideas when the play gets stuck—children love repetition but sometimes they need a little help to get out of a rut

Overrides their grown-up, teacher instincts and feels comfortable sitting on the floor being silly and following their child into places unknown

for infants

The activities in this section for infants focus on imitation. Pretending will not begin until the second year of life, but copying actions sets the stage.

Say It with Gestures: Older infants are ready to use simple gestures to let you know what they want. Demonstrate "all gone," "bye-bye," and "up." As your child approaches her first birthday, demonstrate how to answer the question "How old are you?" by holding up one finger while you say "One!"

» Encourages communication

Clap with Me: Around six to eight months of age, your child will learn to clap. To encourage imitation try this game:

Clap, clap, one, two, three
Clap, clap, clap with me.
Clap, clap, four, and five
Clap, clap, clap, bees in hive.
Clap, clap, six, seven, eight
Clap, clap, clap, you are great.
Clap, clap, nine, and ten
Clap, clap, let's do it again.

» Introduces rhyming and encourages imitation

Bang, Bang Goes the Drum »

When children first begin to imitate your actions, they copy movements they already know. Follow your child's lead and see whether you can get a back-and-forth game going. First he bangs, then you bang, and then everyone bangs together. Create a drum for your child by cutting the bottom out of a coffee can and covering the can with contact paper. Glue plastic lids on each end of the can. You can also improvise by using an empty paper towel roll or an empty oatmeal box.

» Fosters hand-eye coordination and auditory awareness

Can You Stick Out Your Tongue?: Young infants seem to be able to imitate simple facial gestures. Try sticking out your tongue and see whether your baby will follow suit. You can also try opening and closing your mouth to see whether he will copy you.

» **Encourages imitation and back-and-forth conversation**

Follow the Leader: See how many different actions your child can imitate in a row. Tap the table, open and close your hand, clap, wave, and put a hat on your head. Start with actions that your baby is already doing, like banging on a table. Increase the challenge by adding new, multiple, and more complex movements. Be careful not to frustrate your baby, always keeping your attention on your baby's reactions to keep the game fun.

» **Advances imitative skills and memory**

←Can You Stick Out Your Tongue?
Encourages imitation and back-and-forth conversation

for toddlers

For toddlers, pretend activities focus on acting out real-world experiences. Toddlers love to be "just like Mommy and Daddy," and taking on these roles makes them feel more powerful and in control.

Create Your Own Grocery Store: Save empty food boxes and containers. Pudding or tofu boxes work well, as do cereal boxes, small yogurt containers, and empty vitamin bottles. Seal the boxes with tape and attach the lids to the small containers. Store all your "groceries" in a box or laundry basket. Your child will have fun going shopping with a paper bag or small basket. Toddlers have fun filling up bags and baskets with just about anything. For variety and to stretch his imagination, use blocks in place of the groceries.

» Facilitates early pretend play

Happy Birthday to Me: Save some things from your child's first birthday party so he can continue to act out this special day. Use the paper plates, cups, decorations, and candles and have a pretend party with her dolls and stuffed animals.

» Develops imaginative play skills and social awareness

I'll Drive: Ride-in cars that they can scoot with their feet are beloved toys for toddlers. Talk about where your child wants to go. Is he on his way to the beach, to Disney World, or just around the corner to pick up some hamburgers for dinner? He will need keys, some bags, a wallet, and credit cards. Any props that make a child feel grown-up like Mommy and Daddy will be valued.

» Supports pretend play and language skills

→**Create Your Own Grocery Store**
Facilitates early pretend play

Dinner Time! Young children love to play with a pretend kitchen to "prepare" meals. A store bought one is great but you can use side-by-side large sturdy cardboard boxes and fill them with plastic utensils, child-size pots and pans, unbreakable mixing bowls, empty food boxes, and pretend food. Toddlers' imaginative play skills and language are booming, and words like, "hot," "all gone," "cookie," and countless others get real-time practice when you and your child make yummy pretend together.

» **Develops language and imaginative play skills**

Good Night, Baby: Imaginative play is a wonderful way to develop empathy. Baby dolls, for both boys and girls, give children a venue to develop and show love, concern, and tender care. Good night kisses to a cherished doll is a simple and wonderful way for children to be gentle and express affection.

» **Develops empathy and language skills**

Going to Old McDonald's Farm: What toddler doesn't love animals? Keep an array of small and large plastic and stuffed animals around and show your child how to place them in a wagon, toy car or even a shoe box. Drag or push them to the farm singing "Old McDonald" along the way!

» **Develops language, fine and gross motor skills**

Let's Have Tea »

Tea parties are fun at any time of the day. Let your child "pour" and "serve." Don't forget to ask for more "cake." All that tea will make you hungry!

» **Develops social and language skills**

for preschoolers

Preschool pretending becomes more elaborate. As children mature and their language skills increase, their imaginative themes are richer and their stories longer and more complex.

Let's Take a Taxi: Place two chairs side by side and pretend you are the taxi driver. Ask your child where to go, giving suggestions, if needed. Talk about all the things you pretend to see along the way and what you will do when you get there. Put chairs in a line so you can drive a train or pretend you are on an airplane.

» Encourages creative expression

Cleanup Time Can Wait: You don't always have to clean everything up. Find spaces in your home where your child can build freely without needing to clean up at the end of the day. This encourages your child to build more complex creations and facilitates imaginative play.

» Supports creative expression and a sense of pride

Act It Out: Give your child a series of instructions, such as "Can you hop like a rabbit?" "Can you walk like a big, heavy elephant?" "Can you slither like a snake?" Try other animals and include things such as plants growing in the ground, a flower opening on a summer day, or a balloon being filled with air.

» Develops imaginative thinking

Build Forts and Castles: Help your child create special places in which to play. Tents, boxes, blow-up pool rafts, playhouses, cushions, blankets, and sheets can be used to create all kinds of special worlds. This is a perfect activity for your child to do with friends.

» Encourages pretend play and social skills

The Great Outdoors—Inside: Stretch your child's imagination by bringing an outside activity indoors. For example, create a beach using blue towels for the ocean and tan towels for the sand. Your child can make paper fish in the water and help pack a delicious lunch to enjoy on the shore.

» **Supports role-playing and imagination**

Build a Brave New World: There are two types of pretend play. The first is where the child is an actor (he takes on a particular role and acts it out), and the second is where the child is the director. In this type of play your child is the director of a miniature world. He may build the world, make the characters talk, or tell a story about their activities. There are many commercially available play sets and action figures that children can use. Additionally, you can help your child create his own miniature world with blocks, train tracks, cardboard containers, action figures, or miniature animals. Combining different play sets stretches your child's imagination and provides count-less opportunities for expanded pretend play.

» **Fosters imaginative play and creative expression**

→**Build a Brave New World**
Fosters imaginative play and creative expression

alphabet and number games
Promoting Alphabet Skills and Mathematical Thinking

Although your baby is too young for formal school, the foundations for both reading and math skills are developed during the first three years of life. Your child's interest in books, awareness of the magic of the printed word, understanding of stories, and basic vocabulary are important underpinnings for literacy. In these early years, your child will also learn to think mathematically. She will develop a basic understanding of numbers, learn to count, first by rote and then meaningfully, and then develop basic ideas about quantity—more, less, same, different, bigger, and smaller.

Young children who are read to from a young age are more likely to become proficient readers in elementary school. A strong vocabulary at school entrance predicts successful reading and writing. In later years, literacy involves more than mastery of oral language. It requires knowing a lot about books, stories, and print and involves learning to write, which greatly facilitates learning to read.

Children begin to "read" as babies. When their parents read or tell them stories, they enjoy the cadences of language and become familiar with its sounds. They learn to recognize photos of familiar people and objects and also learn to recognize artistic representations. As toddlers, they learn to turn pages in books, look at and name pictures, and follow rituals like patting the bunny or making animal sounds. Soon they can pick out their favorite books by looking at their covers and "read" words of stories they have memorized as they turn the pages.

Two- and three-year-olds get quite good at recognizing printed words that are part of their everyday world. They can find their favorite cereals at the grocery store, recognize the signs and logos of familiar fast food restaurants, and tell you what it says on a stop sign. They may learn to recognize the jerseys of their favorite sports team, push the right button in the elevator, or read the labels on their toys.

Repeated experiences with books help children learn that printed words can tell a story, that we read from left to right, and that the words people see in print correspond with the words they say. Children

Ways to Facilitate Alphabet Skills and Mathematical Thinking

Surround yourselves with books. Children brought up in homes where reading is a priority naturally become good readers.

Make reading a daily habit. Read books with joy and expression.

Ask questions: "What comes next?" "How do you think he feels?" "Where did the boy go?" "Why is he looking for the dog?"

Allow your child to participate in real-world tasks that build number concepts, like setting the table and taking out the right amount of dishes.

Make lists. As your child sees you using the list and crossing off items, she will learn that reading and writing are important and useful skills.

learn that stories have a beginning, a middle, and an end and that events happen in a particular order.

Children learn to imitate reading behaviors before they can actually read. They will hold the book in a certain way, turn the pages one at a time, look at each page, and "read" the story. They will often read to their dolls, incorporating many dramatic elements such as pauses, emphasis, and different voices for different characters. They may also comment on the story they are pretending to read, by saying "that's a good part" or "don't be scared now."

The same is true of writing. Toddlers are thrilled when they first learn to make marks on paper, often gleefully decorating every available surface. As they become preschoolers, they may imitate writing by drawing horizontal lines, scribbling, and labeling their scribbles as writing. They may "sign" their drawings, "write" letters or cards, or make shopping lists. Gradually, their attempts at writing become more intentional and they begin to write real words.

All these skills are key to learning to read and write. Additionally, to read unfamiliar text, children need to "break the code." They need to understand alphabetic principles—that spoken words are made up of individual letters and letter combinations and that written words can be deciphered by sounding out their component parts. They need to master four processes: letter naming, letter sound association, segmentation, and blending.

All of this is, of course, a bit much to expect of a three-year-old, but during these formative years the games we play with our children can lay the groundwork for mastering these processes. Alphabet games, listening games, visual recognition games, storytelling, rhyming games, pretend play that incorporates reading and writing, and of course, plenty of experience being read to all help develop a healthy foundation for literacy.

Children are mathematicians from the day they are born. They are constructing knowledge constantly as they interact mentally, physically, and socially with their environment and other people. Young children may not be able to add, subtract, or multiply, but their interactions with a stimulating environment set the stage for the development of mathematical concepts.

Counting anything, everything, and nothing is a primary preoccupation of the preschool years. Children love counting rhymes and finger plays. They count the steps as they go upstairs and play one, two, three, go! games over and over. Most three-year-olds will learn to count by rote to ten or even higher, but counting by rote is not the same as understanding the mathematical concept of numbers. They must first understand one-to-one correspondence. This means linking one number with each item in a set of objects and understanding that each item can only be counted once.

Children learn number concepts, the foundation of mathematics, gradually over time as they manipulate, explore, and organize materials. Skills important for preschool children include rote counting, one-to-one correspondence, understanding the concept of one and two, comparing amounts (more, less, or same), putting objects in sets of specific numbers, and associating numerals with numbers. Like learning to read, the foundations of math can be developed through everyday experiences and playful games. Once you are aware of the basic progression of mathematical thinking, you can key in to your child's level and provide opportunities that support new understandings.

Characteristics of a Playful Parent

Demonstrates a love of literature

Recognizes that children love repetition—be willing to read and reread the same book; you may get bored, but your child won't

Incorporates number games into daily activities

Plays a variety of music genres.

Respects their child's tolerance and temperament—if children are too active to sit still for a story, there are other ways to keep them engaged in reading. Try holding your child in your arms and telling her stories about the pictures on the wall. You can also read a children's book aloud with a lot of expression. That's a sure way to attract a child to see what you are looking at and reading.

for infants

Although activities for infants are not designed to teach them the alphabet or introduce them to number games, the foundation for these later developments is built in infancy. This is the time to help your baby tune in to the rhythms and cadences of language. Later this will help with phonetic learning when they begin to sound out words. The same is true for number skills. Babies become aware of number concepts as they discover numerical ideas like they have two hands and two feet.

Turn the Page: Introduce simple cardboard books to your child and show her how you turn the pages as you read. As her fine motor skills develop, page turning will become an activity she'll do over and over.
» Encourages imitation and develops an interest in reading

Use Touch and Feel Books: Infants love books that they can touch and feel, such as *Pat the Bunny*. You can also make your own personalized version of this by taking sheets of cardboard or sturdy paper and folding them in half. Using child-safe paste or glue, affix interesting textures like bumpy corrugated cardboard squares and soft silk.
» Develops tactile discrimination and language skills

Thump, Thump, Thump, Bump, Bump, Bump, Jump, Jump, Jump: Saying a simple line of words repetitively gets your baby's ear attuned to the cadences of rhyming. It's an easy way to improvise "songs," and you can use made-up words, too.
» Develops auditory discrimination

I Love Books »

By making reading books a daily occurrence, you help foster a love of literature for your child. Right from birth, gently cradle your infant in your arms and read your favorite books together. This is a special and treasured way to end each day before bedtime—or anytime!

» Sets the stage for a love and appreciation of books

for toddlers

Toddlers love rhymes, naming games, action songs, and, of course, many types of books. Children will now be able to participate more actively in songs with movements, choosing which books they want to read, and engage in conversations.

Revisit Old-Fashioned, Favorite Counting Rhymes:
Introduce your child to lots of interesting counting rhymes, such as:

"This Old Man"
This old man, he played **one, he played knick-knack on my thumb**
With a knick-knack paddy-whack give the dog a bone
This old man came rolling home.
Repeat bold prase and chorus with each subsequent number.
Two, knick-knack on my shoe
Three, knick-knack on my knee.
Four, knick-knack on my door.
Five, knick-knack on my hive.
Six, knick-knack with some sticks.
Seven, knick-knack up to heaven.
Eight, knick-knack on my gate.
Nine, knick-knack on my spine.
Ten, he played knick-knack all over again.
» Develops counting and rhyming skills

Bigger, Smaller, Same, and Different: Develop your child's
awareness of size and shape by pointing out the differences in everyday objects, photos, and picture books.
» Fosters language development and concepts

The Magnetism of Letters »

Although they are not ready to use letters to make words, toddlers love the idea of arranging and rearranging magnetic letters. If your refrigerator is magnetic, it is often the favored place to create letter patterns. They will create patterns by matching colors and shapes even before they can identify them. By observing you when you read words aloud, your toddler may put together random letters and announce a word he has spelled.

» Develops beginning alphabet awareness

« Let's Count

Number awareness begins with the idea that each object is counted only one time. Toddlers love to count their fingers and toes, so show him how to touch each one only once as you count out loud. You can also reinforce this idea that one thing goes in each place by having him put one small ball into each space of a muffin tin.

» **Fosters one-to-one correspondence skills**

Draw in the Salt or Sugar: Fill a shallow tray with salt or sugar. Show your child how to make lines and circles and copy designs. Eventually, he will learn to make letters.

» **Encourages pre-writing skills**

My Name Is Everywhere: One of the first things your child will learn to read is her own name. Provide her with lots of opportunities by labeling clothing, lunchboxes, and school bags. Make a name sign for her bedroom door or make her a special place mat with her name. Talk about the letters.

» **Develops early reading skills**

Count It Out: Toddlers love the idea of counting, and accuracy is not important. Count the stairs as you go up and down, count while you are waiting for the light to turn green, and count the bubbles floating in the air.

» **Introduces basic number skills**

for preschoolers

This is the time to introduce letter games, keeping them fun, short, and tailored to your child's interests. Computer games and electronic games can be fun, but it is through parent-child interaction that your child learns the most.

By the Numbers: Use numbers and number concepts in everyday conversations. Talk about how many days are left until a special event, how many people are coming for dinner, the shapes and sizes of blocks and buildings, or how long a trip will take.

» **Develops mathematical awareness and concept development**

Learn Your Logos: Your child will be on her way to sight-reading when she figures out that a particular design stands for a word. Make a logo book by cutting the logos from newspaper and magazine advertisements or cardboard food containers. Your child is likely to be able to identify the logos from her favorite fast food restaurants, grocery stores, favorite food brands, or stores you frequent.

» **Introduces beginning reading skills**

Match the Letter to the Picture: Write the letters of the alphabet on clothespins. Cut out magazine pictures, one for each letter of the alphabet, and have your child match the clothespin letters to the beginning sounds of the objects in the pictures. Clip the clothespins to the corresponding pictures.

» **Develops alphabet skills**

What's for Lunch »

Involve your child in simple cooking experiences. Let him help as you count out the number of teaspoons of salt that go into the muffins, measure the flour, or make sure that you use twenty strokes to stir the brownies.

» **Encourages mathematical thinking and basic science**

Mind Your P's and Q's (and X's and O's, Too!): This is an easy game you can create to occupy your child while waiting in a restaurant. Print one letter at the top and center of a sheet of paper. Below this, write many letters of the alphabet in no particular pattern, spreading them over the sheet of paper. Have your child circle the letters that match the one printed at the top. Have her place an X over the ones that do not match.

» Fosters letter identification

Keep Moving: Adding movement helps reinforce new learning. Try playing "Mother, May I?" with a focus on number concepts. The object of this game is to be the first to cross the finish line. The leader gives a command, and before a player can execute it, she has to ask, "Mother, may I?" If she forgets, she goes back to the start line. Ask your child to "take three giant steps," "jump forward four times," or make up other fun movements.

» Encourages mathematical thinking, direction following, and motor coordination

scientific thinking
Understanding the World Around Us

Ways to Facilitate Scientific Thinking

Observe the world with your child and comment on what you see.

Encourage experimentation and discovery.

Appreciate learning opportunities in everyday objects and materials.

Go green; teach your child to be a good steward of the planet.

Include your preschooler in chores.

Give your child time to figure things out and don't always supply the answer.

Know the difference between rote memorization and true understanding of a concept.

Provide abundant experience with all types of physical objects.

Right from the beginning, our children approach the world like little scientists. They continually develop new understandings through an ongoing series of experiments, learning and refining their thinking with each new event. When an infant bats at a mobile, sees it flutter, and then bats excitedly to make the flutter happen again, he is displaying scientific thinking. When he bangs a toy loudly on his high chair, then taps it softly and listens to the difference, he is beginning to experiment with the properties of objects and how they relate to each other.

Developing an understanding of the world around us is a lifelong process. As children's ability to reason matures and evolves, they make increasingly logical connections and inferences. This process is a developmental one. Young children do not think in the same way as adults. With experience and feedback, their capabilities expand and they become more logical and abstract. By encouraging an attitude of discovery and supporting our children's innate interest in figuring things out, we set the stage for a lifetime interest in learning.

As children interact with their world, they develop physical knowledge, logico-mathematical knowledge, and social knowledge. Physical knowledge involves learning about objects in the environment and their properties, such as color, size, width, or shape. Logico-mathematical knowledge concerns the relationship among objects as well as their relationships in time and space. Young children are interested in and are discovering numbers, patterning, and sequencing. Social knowledge is conveyed by people and defined by culture. It involves the many social rules, morals, and values children must learn to function in society.

One of the early understandings that children come to is that they can have an effect on the world around them. They cry and someone comes to pick them up, they kick and something jingles, or they press a button and out pops a colorful figure. This rudimentary understanding of cause and effect is important—children are learning how to exercise control over their world.

Because children are thirsty for information as to how the world and their environments work, they are naturally intrigued by finding likenesses and differences and will spend considerable time matching and organizing materials. They love to put all the red things in one basket and blue things in another. Children learn to sort first by the most salient perceptual category: color, shape, or size. As they develop and refine their sorting skills, children learn to sort by more than one attribute. They become increasingly adept at noticing likenesses and differences and arranging things in order. Soon they will learn to put objects in order by size, height, length, and width. They will notice differences in texture and weight and become intrigued by opposites.

There are particular kinds of things that seem to hold the interest of most young children. Children are endlessly fascinated with their own bodies, animals, plants, and the world they live in. Growth and change are all around them and their questions are endless. Children are never too young to begin to learn to appreciate nature and its beauty and to care for and respect our environment.

As parents, we need to understand that knowledge is not something we can just "pour" into our children; rather, it is something that children have to construct for themselves. Acquiring knowledge is an active process in which children continually discover relationships and ideas and refine their worldview based on new information.

This active process of learning takes considerable energy and effort. While we may delight in a child's ability to recite a string of information, like the names of the planets, the months of the year, or the days of the week, memorizing facts does not necessarily translate into true understanding. Reciting the names of the planets may not indicate your child has a notion of outer space. We need to think about what they know, how our children know it, and how we can extend that knowledge.

Characteristics of a Playful Parent

Wonders with their child

Questions but doesn't quiz

Recognizes that it's okay for their child to struggle a little sometimes—by balancing your support with encouraging independent problem solving, you are giving your child boosted self-esteem and tolerance for frustration

Helps their child notice likenesses and differences of things

Makes learning fun and interesting

Follows their child's leads and interests—it is a lot more fun to see how many dinosaurs are in the box than to do rote counting

Learns alongside their child by reading books and investigating different ideas

for infants

Infants are poised to discover many important ideas about the world. They will figure out that their actions cause things to happen and that objects and people still exist even when they cannot be seen. They will gain knowledge of physical properties—some objects are soft, some are hard, for example. The kinds of experiences we provide our infants are designed to help them develop these important concepts—ideas about cause and effect, the ability to anticipate, object permanence, and knowledge of the physical attributes of the world. As children experience the joy of playful experimentation, they develop a strong desire to learn through discovery.

Pots and Pans, So Much To Do!: The simple objects in your kitchen can provide hours of fun for your little one, and the problem-solving challenges are numerous. Pots and pans, particularly if they are shiny, can be more fun than a store-bought toy. Show your baby how to put a lid on the pan. As he gets more accomplished, try giving him two different size pans with lids and see whether he can figure out which lid goes on which pot. You can invent all kinds of hiding games by placing small objects inside the pans and letting your child discover them. Muffin tins are another baby favorite. Tennis balls are just the right size to fit into the holes, creating a homemade puzzle.

» Develops spatial relations and hand-eye coordination

Explore Fabric Collections »

Babies love to feel the texture of materials. Keep a variety of fabric scraps on hand for him to touch and explore in a special box filled with interesting materials of different sizes and colors. Include short ribbons, scarves, pieces of silk, velvet, corduroy, fake fur, and even small pieces of sandpaper. Remember to describe the colors, textures, shapes, and sizes as your baby explores.

» Encourages sensory exploration and language development

The Disappearing Cheerio: As your baby gets close to her one-year birthday, you can create your own version of the old-fashioned shell game. Try hiding a Cheerio under a cup and see whether she can find it. Use two different colored cups and move them around and see whether she remembers which one was the hiding place. After she has found the Cheerio under the first cup, show her you are now putting it under the second cup. See whether she goes to the first cup initially or remembers that this time the game is different.

» **Encourages memory development and attention skills**

Shake, Shake, Shake That Bottle: Partially fill an empty plastic 16-ounce (475 ml) bottle with colored rice or pasta and securely glue the top back on. Your baby will be intrigued by watching what's happening inside as he shakes, rattles, and rolls his shaker.

» **Develops auditory discrimination and fine motor skills**

Lights Out: Let your baby help you turn off the light switch. Before you turn off the light, say, "Lights out." After a while your baby will make the connection between switching off the light and darkening the room.

» **Fosters an understanding of cause and effect**

Sticky Fun: This activity will surprise and mystify your baby. Lay a piece of contact paper on the floor sticky side up and tape the edges down with duct tape so it will remain stationary. Place a variety of small objects on the contact paper and encourage your baby to try lifting them up and putting them back down. Show him what happens when he touches the paper with his hands or bare feet or try putting small bits of Cheerios on the paper and see whether he can retrieve them.

» **Develops fine motor and problem-solving skills**

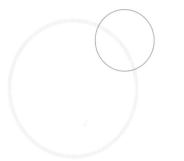

for toddlers

Toddlers are at the age of push, pull, empty, and fill. They are ready to explore their world in new ways. Their growing size and strength as well as their ability to walk provides new ways of acting upon their environment. Activities for toddlers are designed to allow them to make new discoveries about likenesses and differences, how things go together and come apart, as well as new understandings of spatial relationships. This is an age where we introduce puzzles, pegboards, building materials, and pull and push toys.

Clothespin Can: Create a simple puzzle for your child using craft-type clothespins and a coffee can with a plastic lid. Cut a small hole in the lid and show your child how to drop the pins into the coffee can. Remove the lid and let him place the clothespins around the rim.

» **Advances fine motor and problem-solving skills**

Block Tower Play: Build a tower of blocks for your toddler. At this age, the bigger and lighter, the better. Show her how to knock it down and build it back up again. Empty containers, cereal boxes, butter bowls, and cardboard juice containers are perfect for this game.

» **Promotes self-control and spatial awareness**

Follow That Sound: Hide a windup musical toy somewhere in the house and see whether your child can follow the sound and uncover the treasure. Be sure to let your child take a turn hiding the toy for you to discover.

» **Encourages problem-solving and listening skills**

Going on an Egg Hunt: Use inexpensive plastic Easter eggs and an egg carton to make a simple sorting game or puzzle. Choose eggs in three to six different colors. Glue the two parts of the eggs together. Your child will enjoy simply taking the eggs out of the carton and putting them back in. Create a challenge by filling one side of the carton and see whether she can put the matching eggs in the other. You can also color the compartments of the carton to match the eggs and encourage her to put each egg into its correct spot.

» **Advances the development of matching and sorting skills**

What's in the Box »

The slots in tissue boxes are the perfect size for little hands. Your child will love filling, emptying, and refilling the boxes with his favorite small toys. Try stuffing socks or several scarves tied together inside and see whether your child is up to the challenge of pulling them out. Keep the conversation going by expressing your excitement as things disappear and then reappear.

» **Fosters fine motor, problem-solving, and language skills**

All Aboard! Toddler Train: Create a pull train for your child by tying together three different-sized cardboard boxes with string or yarn. Cut small holes in each box and attach them together with a short string. Tie the end of each string around a short piece of plastic straw to prevent the string from pulling through the holes. Tie a small cylindrical wooden black or a small plastic vitamin bottle to the end string to make a handle. Your child will enjoy filling up each car with his stuff and pulling the train behind him wherever he goes.

» **Promotes imagination and concept development**

Beanbag Sort: Young children naturally sort by lining up objects and making distinctions between colors, shapes, and sizes. Provide your child with beanbags of different colors. Tape colored paper in corresponding colors on the floor and encourage your child to sort the beanbags into the corresponding colors.

» **Supports understanding of colors, shapes, and sizes**

Make-It-Fit Puzzles »

Puzzles are used universally to help toddlers with dexterity and problem solving. Rather than simply directing your child to the correct piece, ask questions like, "What color piece are we looking for?" "Is it a big piece or a little piece?" "What if we turn it this way?" Recognizing and encouraging efforts as well as successes helps a child feel proud, capable, and eager to try new things: "You are working so hard on this puzzle!" "You're almost done!"

» **Develops eye-hand coordination and spatial awareness**

for preschoolers

Games and activities for preschoolers are designed to encourage sorting, ordering, and understanding of patterns; awareness of same and different; and understanding of opposites and spatial relationships. Preschoolers are ready to make new connections between objects and to understand ideas about growth and change. They are interested in matching and sorting games. They are ready to talk about differences in size and weight and to learn about categories—some things are alive, some things are not, some things are animals, and some things are plants.

Create an Adventure Walk Collage: Take your child on a nature walk. Collect pebbles, shells, twigs, leaves, and whatever strikes her fancy and bring them home to make a collage. Because many of these items are heavy you will need heavy poster board or oak tag and lots of glue!

» **Fosters an appreciation of nature and encourages an understanding of the properties of objects**

Make a Guess: Preschoolers are skilled at playing guessing games. Two ways to introduce these games that you can apply in different contexts are the games of "What's missing?" and "What's wrong?" "What's missing?" is a game you can play in increasingly sophisticated ways. To begin, take three different colored objects and lay them out in front of your child. Ask your child to close his eyes while you remove one of the objects. Ask him to open his eyes and guess which color you are holding in your hand. You can play this game with a focus on physical properties like color, shape, or size or with a focus on the actual object (the cow is hiding in your hand). Increase the number of items and the complexity of the game over time. Be sure to allow your child to take a turn hiding the objects.

"What's wrong?" is a game that helps a child develop sorting skills. Make a game board that is a 3 by 3-inch (7.5 x 7.5 cm) grid. Cut out three circles (red, green, and yellow), three triangles (red, green, and yellow), and three squares (red, green, and yellow). Put the shapes on the game board in the following pattern:

R G Y (all circles)
R G Y (all triangles)
R G Y (all squares)

Ask your child to close her eyes and while she does switch two of the objects. When she opens her eyes, ask, "What's wrong?" Let her "fix" your mistake. As she masters the concepts involved in solving the puzzle make it more complicated.

» **Supports concept development**

Ping-Pong Blow: Blow through a straw and see whether you and your child can get a Ping-Pong ball to move across the floor or table.

» **Encourages problem solving and discovery learning**

Have Fun with Tape: Create new worlds for your child using colored masking tape. You can create shapes to jump into, roads for cars, and game boards.

» **Expands play opportunities**

Going on a Puzzle Hunt: This is a treasure hunt, counting game, and problem-solving challenge all rolled into one. Take the pieces of a simple favorite puzzle, count them, and then hide them around the house. Have your child count the pieces as he finds them and when he has found all the pieces, put the puzzle back together again.

» **Promotes mathematical thinking and problem solving**

I'm Your Helper: Let your preschooler help you sort the socks when they come out of the dryer. Finding the two that go together is a perfect first matching game. And putting them away helps foster independence and responsibility.

» **Develops classifying skills and encourages responsibility**

Let's Measure: Stock a shoe box with rulers, measuring tape, paper, and pencils. Show your child how to use the tools to see how tall she is and how big Daddy's shoes are in comparison to her sneakers. She can document her findings by taking photos or drawing pictures and writing the number of inches or feet.

Go one step further and put small plastic bowls and measuring spoons and cups in the shoe box. Your preschooler's discoveries will now include a different type of measuring. See how many tablespoons of sand it takes to fill the green bowl, and so on.

» **Develops mathematical thinking**

Smell Jars and Sound Cans: Fill pairs of small plastic containers with different materilas, such as water, rice, or safe-sized rocks. Ask your child to close her eyes and shake them to see if she can match them correctly. Add to the fun by poking holes in the lid of containers and putting cotton balls inside that are lightly saturated with safe scents like vanilla, cocoa powder, and perfume and have her match them.

» **Fosters sensory awareness**

My First Diary: Preschoolers are learning so much each day. A playful way to keep their discoveries interesting and meaningful is to document their findings in journals, through photographs, and through drawing pictures. After a trip to the zoo, for example, she can make a special book of pictures with words to describe what you saw. After his bath time scientific discovery, help him make a graph with columns of which objects sunk and which ones floated with words or drawings under the headers.

» **Supports language, memory, and new understandings of the world**

What Sinks? What Floats?: The bathtub becomes a place for discovery and learning when you introduce the concepts of sinking and floating. Have your child collect waterproof objects from around the house like spoons, plastic bowls, clean rocks, and a variety of toys. Let him guess what will sink and what will stay on the surface of the water before he puts them into his bathwater.

» **Promotes discovery learning**

→**What Sinks? What Floats?**
Promotes discovery learning

making friends

Games and Activities for Developing
Social Skills, Empathy, and Kindness

A critically important, lifelong gift we give our children is how to get along with others. Making friends and demonstrating care and respect are paramount. This learning starts with their very first relationship with caring adults and then extends to the other important people in their lives. Babies, as young as three months old, are interested in watching people and are fascinated with other children. Toddlers squeal with joy when their favorite friends show up, and although they are still navigating interactions with other children, they are clearly developing the roots of friendship building.

Mastering social skills takes time and experience. Cooperation begins in infancy with the kinds of turn-taking games parents naturally do as they play with children: You roll the ball to baby, and she rolls it back. Your child playfully drops a toy and you pick it up. Baby offers you a bite of her cookie and you say, "Thank you!" Through these simple experiences, children are learning the basics of social interchanges.

One of the hallmarks of making friends is the ability to empathize, or understand what another person is feeling. Toddlers can exhibit considerable empathy and adjust their behaviors in response to the feelings of other children and adults. You can see this when your toddler gives you a hug when you look sad or when she gives her baby doll a "bottle." Because empathy is a skill that must be taught, it is critically important for adults to demonstrate acceptance, respect, and understanding toward others and model loving relationships.

Playing together is a developmental process. Toddlers tend to play happily next to friends but don't actually play *with* them. Preschoolers have more complex interactions. They delegate, share, determine themes, and build together. Some children take naturally to playing with others and enjoy the company of their peers while others find it much more difficult to accept new people. Sometimes it's easier to play with another child on neutral territory where children do not have to feel possessive of their own toys. Meeting at a playground where children can run and climb together without worrying about sharing toys is often a great way to introduce new friends.

Ways to Facilitate Social Skills Development

Give your child the opportunity to interact with children of different ages.

Set up the environment so that play is fun and successful with age-appropriate toys.

Choose toys that encourage two children to play together.

Model the use of words to describe feelings, such as "I get sad when the pages are ripped out of the book" or "I feel so happy when you give me kisses."

Encourage and model helping others for your child.

Just as walking and talking are developmentally sensitive, so are the social skills that children learn. We would not expect a six-month-old to take her first steps, nor should we expect an eighteen-month-old to willingly relinquish his favorite toy to another toddler. Sharing and taking turns do not come easily to most young children. Toddlers are self-centered and have a difficult time understanding why they must give up a favorite toy or wait to take a turn. Even learned skills can easily come undone when a child is tired, hungry, or stressed, and tantrums can occur over a seemingly small event between two children.

It is the wise parent who sets up the environment for a visiting friend by putting away her daughter's treasured stuffed bunny rabbit and offers a variety of toys that are meant to be shared, such as blocks, paper and crayons, and balls. Short playtime visits with successful outcomes are the way to go.

As children get older, their repertoire of social skills are strengthened and having friends over becomes a favorite activity with more sophisticated play. Although altercations will still occur over who had the purple marker first, preschoolers are able to resolve conflicts easier than before, and friends are important and treasured.

Children develop empathy and social skills by observing the reactions of others around them. Throughout the day, many natural interactions, such as being gentle with pets, kissing a boo-boo, or patting a baby doll gently to sleep, help expand and reinforce skills. Modeling these behaviors for young children helps them develop these skills, so modulating your own emotions is extremely important. By expressing a range of feelings respectfully and carefully, you will be helping your young child internalize values about responding to others, considering the way others feel, and participating in healthy relationships with others.

The nuances of play and making friends are both subtle and complex. What might seem like a simple interaction with your child is actually multilayered. Your toddler or preschooler needs to be enticed and interested in an activity or interaction. Playful parents are sensitive to this and are aware of the "dance" number that you and your child do. You consider your child's temperament, activity level, and interests. Sometimes you can excitedly present a toy; other times you can begin playing with the toy yourself while your cautious toddler observes. Engaging a young child in the process takes time and sensitivity.

Another level of social interaction skill building concerns the way our children interact with others. Parents who model kindness and empathy teach valuable lessons. Additionally, it is vital to know when to step in and when to allow children to work things out with less support. Friendship building takes time and multiple experiences, so provide many opportunities for your child to play with others.

When asked what you want your child to be when he grows up, it is most likely you will answer, "I want him to be happy." By fostering social skills, you will be helping your child in all facets of his life.

Characteristics of a Playful Parent

Demonstrates respect and kindness to friends and family

Models conflict resolution

Uses humor and a playful attitude when things get challenging

Uses positive discipline

Gives their child responsibilities to encourage a sense of pride and confidence

for infants

For infants, developing social skills involves learning the joy of playing with trusted caregivers, especially Mommy and Daddy. Even at this young age babies learn to "tune" in to social cues and figure out how to get your attention and engage you in play.

Let's Take Turns: Simple games such as "I roll the ball to baby, he rolls it back to me," set the stage for turn taking. This is an important skill that will be expanded with maturity and will help toddlers and preschoolers navigate playful interactions with friends.

» **Encourages social skills**

Sharing with the Cookie Monster: When your baby is old enough to handle healthy and safe finger foods, start asking for a bit. Watch as your child playfully hands you her cookie or even a sip of her treasured bottle. This activity sets the roots of sharing and caring.

» **Facilitates empathy**

Create a Comfort Zone: When your baby is crying, use words to label both how you think she is feeling and what you are going to do to soothe her. The conversation may sound like this: "Katie, you are crying because you want Mommy to hold you. I'm going to pick you up as soon as I put the cup down."

» **Encourages emotional awareness**

Make Nice »

Teaching your infant about caring for others can start with the basic "make nice." Show your child how to gently stroke your hair, his big brother's face, or your puppy's fur to teach him to care about others.

» **Faciliates empathy**

for toddlers

The egocentric, it's-all-about-me toddler needs many opportunities to become comfortable playing with others. Treat people the way you would like your child to treat them. Your impressionable child is watching everything you do and listening to everything you say. The best way to ensure that your child will be polite and respectful is to always be a good role model.

Let's Play!: When you invite a friend over for a playdate, don't expect the two children to just go off and play. They may need your help to get the play started. One trick that often works is to begin playing yourself.
» **Develops social skills**

Explore Hands-on Fun: A great way to encourage your toddler to be comfortable with a friend is to engage them both in a sensory activity. Water play, sand play, shaving cream fun, or playing with clay both relaxes children and allows them to play together without the stress of sharing a favorite toy.
» **Supports friendship making**

All about Me: This is the perfect age to create a homemade book about your child and her family. After you collect photographs of treasured people, pets, and objects and add simple words to label and describe, you can "publish" your book by covering the pages with clear contact paper to preserve it.
» **Advances social awareness**

A Day in the Life: Add to your homemade book collection by creating a book that has photographs showing all the terrific things your toddler can do. Take pictures of things such as him eating breakfast, brushing his teeth, playing ball, feeding his fish, and watering his plants. Keep adding pages to the book, and you will have a true best seller.

» **Facilitates self-awareness**

Visits with My Special Friends: Toddlers are just beginning to figure out the nuances of friendships. Give your child a shoe box that she can decorate with markers, crayons, pasted-on pictures, and stickers. Fill the box with photos of her friends, family, and pets. Give her access to the box and let her go through the photos. Talk about the pictures, such as how much fun that day at the park was, when she is going to play with her friend again, and how much she loves her grandma.

» **Facilitates social relationships**

Come and Play: Practice makes perfect. The more opportunities your toddler has to play with friends, the better developed her social skills will be. Sometimes parents begin to avoid play dates because their child has such a difficult time sharing. In actuality, keep the playdates coming and plan ahead by putting away special toys and replacing them with toys and activities that are the most fun played with two children. Great ideas include Play-Doh, art activities, motor games, block building, and sensory fun. Also, keep the playdate short so you can end on a happy note.

» **Encourages friendships**

→**Come and Play**
Encourages friendships

for preschoolers

Preschoolers love friends. They talk about who is their best friend and prefer friends even more than they do some of their favorite adults. When children have a strong foundation of empathy, kindness, and respect, other children will seek them as a playmate.

Stop! Go!: Play games that involve starting and stopping, such as "Red Light, Green Light." Developing a sense of self-control is an important skill helps children negotiate, compromise, and work out conflicts without losing their temper.

» Encourages self-control

I Can Do It!: Create a chart of the various "jobs" that your child is responsible for. Take pictures of your preschooler making his bed, putting away his toys, or setting the table. A visual reminder works for your child like your plan book; it helps remind him of what needs to be done and how to do it. Keep jobs simple and offer support when needed.

» Encourages independence

Meet New People: Expand your child's social circle by including children and adults of different ages and cultures. When you model respect for others and extend good manners, your child will learn the same.

» Expands social skills

Snack Time, Social Time: Just as it is with grownups, sitting down at a table to snack with a friend will encourage your preschooler to strike up a conversation. Serve a simple snack that you know they will both enjoy.

» Encourages relationship building

Taking Care of Others »

Being responsible and sensitive to the needs of others fosters empathy and kindness. Watering plants produces extra reinforcement when your garden includes vegetable plants and fruit trees. Caring for cats, dogs, hamsters, and even frogs or fish teaches children important lessons. To help your child become responsible, give her simple tasks, such as giving food and water to pets. As your child matures, her responsibilities can increase.

» Fosters responsibility

laugh with me
Games and Activities for Promoting a Sense of Humor

Who can resist the deep belly laugh of a baby or the out-of-control laughter of a preschooler? Seeing what is silly and funny is a wonderful trait, and parents play an important role in helping their children develop a sense of humor. Children begin to observe social patterns at a very young age. This is an important skill because it helps infants, toddlers, and preschoolers make sense of their world and recognize what is to come next. These patterns appear in everything we do, such as the way we sing songs, the order in which we get our children dressed, and even how we say our words. Without realizing it, we are teaching our children about these patterns from the moment they are born by doing things in the same ways over and over again. It is when we change these patterns and introduce something unexpected that we first see children react with humor.

Think about your child's personality, temperament, and style and how he reacts in situations. Some children are easygoing and ready to tackle the world from a very young age. They are usually unfazed by strangers and happy to be in new environments. Other children are slow to warm and require gentle introductions to new people, places, and things. Then there is the fussier child who is difficult to soothe and may need a lot of attention. Accordingly, each of these types of children will react differently to changes in social patterns and therefore to the way they determine whether things are funny.

A robust baby will love a colorful and noisy jack-in-the-box. He may startle, then laugh when jack pops up, and show you he wants more. A more sensitive baby may startle, then cry. Likewise, your preschooler may think it's so funny to have Mommy "lose" her glasses when in fact they are on her head. Or your preschooler may need a bigger, more robust "trick" to get a rise.

Humor between parents and children helps promote attachment and healthy emotional development. So laugh away! The obvious rule of thumb is to have fun. Not only will it be enjoyable for everyone, but humor also helps defuse frightening and frustrating situations for you and your child. Laughter is, indeed, often the very best medicine.

Ways to Encourage a Sense of Humor

Give your child lots of opportunities to see things from different perspectives.

Change routines and patterns to help children see what's different and funny.

Embrace your silly side and find the humor in everyday moments.

Model a positive outlook with humor and acceptance even when things are challenging or frustrating.

Appreciate and respect the unique personality of your child.

Accept and support your children's humorous take on things.

Have special "inside" jokes with the family.

for infants

Always watch your baby's reactions to determine whether he loves the game or is overwhelmed by it. For a young infant, that would mean turning his head away, crying, fussing, or appearing frightened. A sense of humor is a learned trait and it takes time to develop.

Let's Get Silly: Once your baby hears the same words repeatedly, he will see the humor in a change of tempo, volume, or pronunciation. Another way to get silly is to make up words and combine them with fun gestures, such as quickly raising your hands in the air and saying "Whoosh!"

» Encourages the beginning of a sense of humor

Jelly Belly: Nothing gets a baby going better than tickly belly kisses. If your baby is ready, you can add loud kisses and "raspberries."

» Encourages laughter and sharing of special moments

Where Am I?: There's a reason why peek-a-boo has been around for centuries—children love it. At first, just covering your face with your hands may get a reaction. As your infant matures, you can cover your head with a giant hat or scarf and quickly remove it to get the giggles going.

» Promotes giggles and an understanding of object permanence

Jack-in-the-Box »

The surprise pop-up can be startling or humorous. Watch your baby's reaction to determine how ready she is for this favorite toy. If you don't have a wind-up one, you can use a shoe box with a hole cut out of the bottom. A puppet can pop out of the top to get the same reaction.

» Facilitates fun through anticipation and surprise

for toddlers

Toddlers' expanding humor repertoire lets them understand that it is funny when things are out of order or when objects are used for things other than what they are intended for. Most significantly, this age absolutely adores when silly Daddy makes up crazy-sounding words or when Mommy chases and tickles them. It's a wonderful stage, and humor can be used to distract and redirect an uncooperative toddler.

Sing a Silly Song: Toddlers love music and the sillier the song, the better. Change words, find great songs that have silly themes, and make up your own special songs with lyrics just for your child. Try the following favorite:

"On Top of Spaghetti"
On top of spaghetti all covered with cheese
Ryan lost his poor meatball when somebody sneezed
It rolled off the table and onto the floor
And then Ryan's meatball rolled out of the door!
» **Supports a sense of humor through music**

Socks on Hands, Shoes on Head: Getting dressed in the morning may be a chore with an uncooperative toddler, but add some humor and it will be the highlight of the day.
» **Facilitates fun in everyday moments**

Books, Books, and More Books »

It's no surprise that reading books is simply one of the best activities for you and your toddler. Because this age loves to hear the same book a zillion times, they will get to know every page, picture, and word. Change things up by telling the story in a different, funny way and watch your child's reaction to see whether he gets the humorous change.

» **Supports a joy of reading**

Enjoy Breakfast for Dinner: Change things up by letting go of solid routines. Your toddler will love having a breakfast meal like pancakes and scrambled eggs for dinner and can help you think of other silly things to do. Once in a while, have a special treat like eating ice cream first or putting soup in Daddy's coffee cup instead of a bowl.

» **Develops a sense of humor**

Catch Me If You Can: As your toddler becomes mobile, he loves to be chased. Darting around furniture and down the hallways while declaring "I'm going to get you!" is a surefire way to get laughs.

» **Encourages a sense of humor while developing motor skills**

←Catch Me If You Can
Encourages a sense of humor while developing motor skills

for preschoolers

The increasingly sophisticated preschooler is now ready to "get the joke." They love to be silly and see the humor in almost everything they do and observe. Be prepared for outrageous and sometimes gross humor that preschoolers get a kick out of.

Read Me a Story: Start a story and have you and your preschooler go back and forth every few sentences to finish it. You can take dictation and make it into a book that your child can illustrate—the sillier, the better.

» **Facilitates imaginative thinking and beginning reading skills**

Early Bathroom Humor: It may be a challenge to accept it, but preschoolers love off-color humor. So making fart sounds under their arms, tooting into empty paper towel rolls, and telling ridiculous jokes are all part of this age. Appreciate it, accept it, and go with the flow.

» **Encourages a sense of silliness**

Express Yourself: Let your child's inner van Gogh come out with an array of magazine photos you've cut out together. Cut out and then glue down on a big circle different noses, eyes, hair, and so on to make funny creatures.

» **Fosters creativity**

« Lights! Camera! Action!

Keep a box of dress-up clothes filled with interesting items. Include hats, jewelry, shoes, clothing, and a potpourri of treasures. Play dress-up together and make up stories about your new "characters." Do it in front of a mirror and if you have a video camera, tape yourselves for later giggles.

» **Fosters role-playing and imagination**

Experiment with Funky Food: Put out lots of interesting and healthy things to eat and let your preschooler make up his own funky recipe. Make smoothies with bananas, apple juice, and carrots! Have a salad with lettuce, tomatoes, and corn chips! Nothing tastes better than a recipe that is both made by him and so silly, too.

» **Fosters independence and healthy eating habits**

Come Up with Crazy Questions: Ask your child silly "yes or no" questions. Do pigs fly? Do elephants bark? Does Daddy have three heads?

» **Develops thinking skills and creativity**

icky, sticky fun
Fostering Creativity and Sensory Awareness

Children explore the world around them through their senses. They touch, taste, shake, rattle, and pound! For young children, sensory exploration is inextricably linked to learning. For them, everything is hands-on, and fine-tuning their ability to explore through their senses helps deepen their understanding of the world around them.

Infants are keenly sensitive to sensory information from the moment of birth, and they use new information to learn. By giving your baby a variety of experiences where she can touch a plethora of textures, you help her learn about her world. Touching sand, feeling the cut blade of grass on her feet, and holding cold spaghetti feed her natural desire to explore.

As your baby's fine and gross motor skills progress, he will become an active experimenter, trying out new ways of playing and interacting. He wants to touch and taste all kinds of novel things.

Toddlers continue this worldly exploration. Most love to get messy, touching, tasting, smearing, pouring, and emptying everything they can get their hands on. They become engrossed in drawing and painting even though they are not particularly interested in the outcome. Eventually, preschoolers turn their attention to how their creations look. They are proud of their drawings, paintings, and sculptures and enjoy artistic exploration.

Exploration is the wellspring of creativity. When we provide a wide range of sensory experiences, we encourage children to make new connections and think in new ways. Children are natural scientists; they are also natural artists. When they are given the time, materials, and freedom, their creativity can be boundless.

Ways to Encourage Sensory Exploration

Provide your child with the opportunity to experiment with a variety of materials of different textures and consistencies.

Give your child experiences with rhythm, melody, and movement.

Engage all your child's senses—touch, taste, smell, sight, and hearing—through playful games and interactions.

Tolerate some mess.

Keep art materials organized in ways that make it easy for children to access them.

Proudly displays your child's artwork and creations.

Focus on the process rather than the product.

for infants

Activities for infants are designed to invite exploration. Provide your baby with a variety of sensory materials to look at, listen to, touch, taste, and manipulate to enhance her interest in making new discoveries.

Brrrr . . . It's Cold!: Place some ice cubes on the tray of her high chair. She will delight in watching them slip and slide around. Once the ice melts and is small enough to fit into your baby's mouth, remove it and replace with fresh large cubes.

» Facilitates sensory awareness

Spaghetti Pull: Try putting several strands of wet cooked spaghetti on your infant's high chair tray. He will love the slippery feel and the challenge of getting some pasta into his hands and mouth.

» Facilitates creative exploration

Squish, Mush, and Push: Mix a few tablespoons of powdered tempera paint into ¼ cup (60 ml) of liquid laundry starch. Pour the mixture into a zip-top bag and seal it securely. Double bag it to ensure that it doesn't spill or puncture. Show your baby how to push on it to create interesting effects.

» Develops problem-solving and thinking skills

Blowing Bubbles »

Babies love watching streams of bubbles float through the air. Once they become mobile, chasing the bubbles and catching and popping them becomes even more fun. Look for bubble containers that are non-spill and have pop-up wands.

» Develops tracking skills

« Get Corny

Cornmeal has an interesting texture and it's easy to clean up once the inevitable spills occur. Put a small amount in a baking pan and let your baby experiment with the way it feels.

» Develops tactile discrimination

Follow the Bouncing Ball: A simple flashlight can be a great toy. You can start by letting your baby track the light as you move it back and forth and up and down across his field of vision. When he is able to sit up, shine the light in various places around the room and see whether he can follow the movements. When he's walking, it's even more fun because he can chase the light as it moves around. Shine it on a wall or ceiling in a dark room. You can add even more interest by creating colored filters out of balloons. Try using more than one colored flashlight to create a dancing rainbow.

» Fosters visual and motor skills

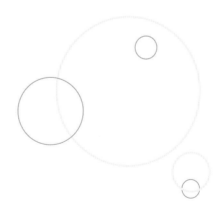

for toddlers

Toddlers enjoy playing with a wide variety of sensory materials—water, sand, and mud all provide unlimited possibilities. This is also the time to introduce art activities, supporting creative exploration while at the same time helping develop fine motor skills that will be important for writing.

Enjoy the Sands of Time: Sand play can work indoors and provide hours of fun. Clean sand is available at most toy stores or hardware stores, and you don't need to fill up an entire sandbox.

Fill a small tub or basin with sand and give your child a variety of implements. For some children the fun is playing with action figures and creating their own miniature worlds and scenarios, while others enjoy the sensory experience of using funnels, cups, and shovels, focusing on pouring and building sandcastles. You can experiment with making the sand a bit damp and seeing how it facilitates the play. Try filling a squeeze bottle with colored water and let your child squeeze the water into the sand to make designs.

» Develops creativity and imagination

Painting without Staining: For a no-mess painting experience that exercises your child's imagination and large muscles, try giving your little one a real paintbrush and a bucket of water and in true Tom Sawyer fashion, show her how to paint the fence.

» Encourages creative and gross motor skills

Cook Up Some Fun with Dough: This is a perennial favorite for most children. You can use commercially available Play-Doh or make your own. Be creative about the kinds of implements you provide for play. Cookie cutters, rolling pins, stamping implements, and action figures are all good possibilities. Don't introduce everything at once; provide different materials on different days to keep the play exciting.

» **Develops fine motor skills and imaginative play**

Squeeze and Squash: Gelatin has a unique bouncy texture. Make the recipe according to the directions on a box of unflavored gelatin but reduce the amount of liquid by half. Pour into a pan and after chilling, cut into cubes. These mini "blocks" can be stacked and squished to your child's delight.

» **Develops fine motor skills and sensory awareness**

Strike Up the Band: Make homemade instruments! Put uncooked rice inside a cardboard tube and securely cover both ends to make a shaker. Put beans inside two paper plates stapled together. Pot lids make great cymbals and cardboard containers can be great for drums. Here are some other ideas:

Sandpaper blocks: Cover blocks with sandpaper and strike them against one another.
Horns: Find a variety of funnels and discover the sounds you can make.
Maracas: Fill plastic bottles with beans and tape the lids tightly.
Drums: Oatmeal containers and spoons work perfectly.
Strike up the family band!

» **Encourages creativity and listening skills**

« Homemade Play Dough

This simple recipe makes smooth silky dough that can last for several weeks when placed in the refrigerator in a sealed plastic bag.

2 cups (250 g) flour
1 teaspoon cream of tartar
1 cup (290 g) salt
2 tablespoons (28 ml) oil
2 cups (475 ml) water
1 teaspoon food coloring

Combine all the ingredients in a medium-size saucepan and stir constantly over medium heat until thoroughly mixed. If children are involved in making the dough, always supervise this activity.

« Paint on a Large Canvas

There are all kinds of interesting ways to finger paint. Children love large surfaces, so this can be done on a table, a tiled floor, large trays, cookie sheets, or a commercially available "messy" play tray. Don't worry about using paper; it's really the process that's fun. If your child wants to save his or her work, just take a piece of construction paper and make a print. Finger paint on a cookie sheet with plain shaving cream or add some drops of food coloring for special fun.

» **Develops fine motor skills and creativity**

Bag It: Fill a zip-top freezer bag halfway with a sensory material such as mud, pudding, or hair gel. Superglue it shut and place it inside a second bag for extra strength. Let the no-mess fun begin!

» **Develops fine motor skills**

Roll It On: Fill a clean roll-on deodorant bottle, the kind with a ball roller, with tempera paint for a new way to roll out colors. Your child can paint on a variety of surfaces like paper, white boards, or even the sidewalk. Providing these different places to paint plus offering plentiful colors will give your child new experiences as a budding artist.

» **Encourages creativity**

Funtastic Paint: You can turn any wall of your home into a chalk wall by painting it with several coats of blackboard paint, which is available in paint and hardware stores. As your child matures and his fine motor skills improve, you can move from large chunky chalk to smaller pieces.

» **Develops fine motor and beginning writing skills**

Stamp Out Some Fun: To create interesting sponge prints, cut sponges into a variety of shapes. Pour a thin layer of tempera paint into a small tray and show your toddler how to stamp the colors onto a sheet of paper. You can also use recycled objects to paint with, such as old hairbrushes, strings, and jar tops.

» **Develops hand-eye coordination and creativity**

Messy Art: Crumple up pages from a newspaper, a magazine, or use wrapping paper, and let your child dip it into nontoxic paint and then onto a large piece of paper. Keep everything on the floor so that your child can get messy and have fun.

» **Develops creativity and fine motor skills**

Rainbow Lunch Bags: Toddlers love to carry things around. Provide a rainbow array of crayons, paints, brushes, glue, and paper scraps to decorate lunch size paper bags. Once dry, your toddler can fill his special bag with all sorts of goodies…even his lunch!

» **Develops creativity and fine motor skills**

Finger Paint Fun: Let your child spread corn syrup on a piece of cardboard. Use a small paint brush or an eye dropper to put drops of nontoxic food coloring onto the paper. Let your child use the brush or her fingers to smear the colors all around to make a beautiful picture. Food coloring stains so dress accordingly.

» **Develops creativity and fine motor skills**

Shake It Up »

Large plastic soda bottles can be turned into a great sensory activity. Create a bubble bottle by filling the bottle three-quarters of the way with water and adding 3 tablespoons (45 ml) of dish soap. For a wave bottle, fill the bottle two-thirds of the way with water and add 3 tablespoons (45 ml) of cooking oil. For a slow-motion bottle, fill it with shampoo or corn syrup. Add glitter for sparkle. Make them your child's favorite colors by adding drops of food coloring and be sure to seal the bottles well.

» **Encourages creativity and thinking skills**

for preschoolers

The preschool years are a time where almost all children love art activities and the messier, the better. Clay, paint, crayons, glue, and paper are just some of the materials that will give hours of creative fun for your child. Relax and enjoy!

Yummy Dough: Guaranteed to provide hours of fun, this dough is also delicious. This recipe creates a concoction that feels just like store-bought Play-Doh. It can be pounded, stretched, cut into pieces, rolled out, and of course, eaten! Give your child all kinds of different kitchen implements to make the play interesting.

Peanut Butter Play Dough*
This is a twist on a fun dough recipe.
1 cup (260 g) smooth peanut butter
1 cup (340 g) corn syrup
1 ½ cups (180 g) confectioners' sugar
1 ½ cups (195 g) powdered milk
Combine all the ingredients in a medium-size bowl and mix until it becomes the texture of clay.
*Ask parents of playmates about peanut allergies before using.
» **Develops creativity and imagination**

Make Goop: Mix equal parts liquid laundry starch and glue to create smooth, white, stretchy silly putty–like clay that can be drawn on with markers.
» **Develops creativity and imagination**

All the News That's Fit to Paint: Sometimes it's fun to paint on a very large surface. Cover a table with sheets of newspaper or newsprint and let your child create a masterpiece with crayons, markers, and paint.

» **Develops creativity and imagination**

Mix It Up: Preschoolers love gluing anything and everything and the more glue, the better. Try using glue sticks or paste. Keep boxes of collage materials available. Try magazines for cutting out pictures. Use pieces of string, beads, stickers, tissue paper, napkins, paper towels, wallpaper, scraps of fabric, yarn, buttons, beans, macaroni, seeds, leaves, twigs, shells, feathers, bottle caps, straws, and cotton balls.

» **Encourages creativity and fine motor skills**

Blowin' in the Wind: Put a blob of thin tempera paint on a piece of paper and show your preschooler how blowing the puddle of paint creates interesting effects.

» **Encourages thinking skills**

Ice Cube Fun: Place a sheet of paper in the bottom of a baking pan and sprinkle it with tempera paint. Place an ice cube in the pan and let your child rotate it around to make an interesting design. You can substitute powdered drink mix or gelatin powder for the powdered tempera paint.

» **Develops creativity and sensory awareness**

Paint with Music: Play different kinds of music while your child paints. Try fast-paced and slow music and a variety of musical styles and see how your child reacts as she creates to the rhythms.

» **Encourages creative expression**

« Sprout Some Veggie Stamps

Make a variety of stamps from cut-up pieces of raw potatoes, broccoli, cauliflower, and carrots. Dipping the stamps into paint and making prints on paper creates incredibly interesting designs.

» **Develops fine motor skills and creative expression**

Happy Birthday to You: The next time your child gives a birthday gift, wrap it in paper she makes herself. Here's a fun way for your young child to make gift wrap. Crumple newspaper into a ball and dip it in paint. Press the newspaper ball lightly over plain paper using a number of colors. Let it dry and wrap the gift. Children get special joy by making cards for their friends and family. Keep a box filled with art supplies like markers, crayons, pencils, ribbon, glue, glitter, tape, and colored construction paper. Preschoolers love to sign their names and as their dexterity improves, they will start to write messages and draw pictures on their cards.

» **Develops social skills and beginning writing**

Create a Frosty Masterpiece: Beat or whisk 1/2 cup (120 ml) of cold water and 1 cup (115 g) of powdered laundry soap together until stiff. Let your child add drops of his favorite color of food coloring into the mixture. Have fun making a three-dimensional picture on heavy paper or cardboard. Let his masterpiece dry flat.

» **Develops creativity and sensory awareness**

Salad Spinner Art: Use an old salad spinner for this art project. Take out the plastic insert and place a paper plate in the bottom of the spinner. Put the insert back, dribble paint into the spinner, put the lid on, and spin to get a beautiful painting.

» **Fosters artistic expression**

Homemade Rainbow Crayons: Don't throw away those broken crayons. Remove any paper from the crayons and place the broken bits in a nonstick muffin tin; put the tin in the oven on very low heat to melt. Check frequently and let cool. These crayons are beautiful and easy for little hands to hold! For easy cleanup, use paper muffin liners.

» **Encourages hand-eye coordination**

Play Activities and Ideas for Making Life with Your Child Fun and Hassle-Free

play begins at home

Playing with your child fosters a close and healthy relationship and can save the day when times get stressful or boring. Every minute of every day also offers myriad learning opportunities. Teachable moments abound even during what appears to be a mundane experience. Playful parents see the magic in these everyday moments and use these times to expand their child's sense of wonder and discovery.

Here are tips for daily activities and routines that are fun for both you and your child. Use these helpful strategies at home and when you are out and about. Playful parenting helps circumvent challenging situations and makes being a mom or dad a lot easier and certainly more enjoyable.

soothing and calming

Nothing is more frustrating for a new parent than not being able to soothe a crying baby. For the very youngest of babies, there are some simple techniques that are surprisingly effective. Many babies are disconcerted when they are startled by a loud noise or when their arms and legs flail during a crying jag. Safely swaddling them in a soft blanket can be very reassuring to a newborn baby.

An age-old trick used by many parents to soothe crying sleepless babies is a car ride or an infant swing. Often equally effective is rocking your baby gently from side to side while on her tummy in your arms (be sure to turn her onto her back if she falls asleep). Making a shushing sound close to your baby's ear is incredibly helpful as well.

We can help our babies learn how to soothe themselves. Pacifiers work wonders for many infants and toddlers, but oftentimes babies don't take to them right away. You may need to gently give your child short opportunities to learn to suck on the pacifier or try multiple kinds until you find the perfect one. Children can become attached to a favorite silky blanket or a soft stuffed toy and find it very comforting.

Older babies and toddlers are still grappling with ways to gain self-control. A toddler having a tantrum may be upsetting to you but it is equally upsetting and scary for your child. The best way to handle a tantrum is to avoid it in the first place. Make decisions about what is truly important to you. Pick your battles and understand the limits of your young child's capabilities. Young children are going to spill their juice, have toileting accidents, and object to sharing their favorite toys.

When you understand how much growth and development is going on in your toddler's brain, it becomes clearer as to why he falls apart when his sandwich is cut into triangles instead of rectangles. Young children do not yet have a good method to handle change and transitions. Such things seem relatively minor from an adult perspective, but to a small child they can be earth shattering.

Here is where a playful parent can successfully avoid escalating the hysterics. Distraction works wonders, silliness helps, patience is golden, and ignoring the tantrum shows your child that his hysteria won't get him what he wants. In spite of your best efforts, sometimes tantrums are unavoidable. You may just have to pick up your screaming toddler and leave the park.

Preschoolers have a better handle on ways to cope with challenges and stresses. Their locus of self-control is more developed, and they have learned, mostly by watching you, how to deal with a dropped ice cream cone or your refusal to buy a toy. That's not to say that your four-year-old won't fall apart when things become just too much to handle. Although her sense of humor is delightfully advanced now, it may actually be hard to distract her from a meltdown with a silly approach. Instead, practice things like deep breathing, visualizing, and counting to 10 (or 20 if necessary) during the calm moments. By making these tools second nature, it is easier for your child to access them during stressful times.

Tips for Soothing and Calming

The 5 S's: Five simple steps that trigger the calming reflex include swaddling, side/stomach position, shushing, swinging, and sucking, according to *The Happiest Baby on the Block*, by pediatrician Harvey Karp, MD. Karp's book and DVD have been a lifesaver for many new parents because these simple yet effective methods work so well when calming a fussy baby.

Lullaby and Goodnight: Music soothes the soul, and quiet classical music is particularly effective. Start playing the music a few minutes before bedtime or naptime and after a while your child will begin to associate its calming effects with drifting off to sleep.

Silly Nilly: When times get stressful, sometimes the easiest and most effective strategy is to be silly. When your child doesn't want to get into the car seat, pretending that you're going on an elephant ride, for example, can turn an objection into a smile.

Exercise: Children need to move. Just like adults, children fare best when they exercise, so give them lots of opportunities to run, jump, and play outdoors. Of course, the weather may not always cooperate, so don't ignore the possibilities of indoor exercise. Setting up your own home gym is easy. An exercise mat and some upbeat music, along with your participation in a "workout routine," may be all you need. You and your child can also take the pillows off the couches and make a great obstacle course.

Take a Break: When times get stressful, the best strategy may be to take a break. For your infant or toddler, find a change of scenery. For your preschooler, put away that puzzle that seems too difficult complete.

Practice Healthy Habits »

Simple yoga poses are a great introduction for preschoolers to the practice of relaxation and a wonderful way to get in the habit of exercising together. There are a number of books and DVDs on yoga with children you can use to get started.

Simple Games for Soothing and Calming

Mad, Sad, Happy, Glad: Identifying children's emotions gives them a vocabulary to describe their feelings. Cut out pictures from magazines and make a "feeling" collage or create a book called "Things That Make Me Happy" or "Things That Make Me Sad."

Bam! Let It Out!: Hitting a punching ball or a pillow gives your child a safe way to release her anger and pent-up feelings. See who can hit it the hardest, try counting the punches, or add silly sound effects.

Use a Balloon: Deep breathing is an effective way to calm down. Get a Mylar balloon and ask your child to try to blow it across the room. For older preschoolers, ask them to pretend they are blowing up a balloon as they breathe deeply and exhale.

Toes to Nose: When children are tense or frustrated or can't fall asleep, a good way to teach them to self-soothe is by practicing simple relaxation techniques. Show your child how to tense and release each body part as you move from her toes to her legs, tummy, arms, hands, and face. Use a soothing voice when doing this exercise. This game also works wonders when your preschooler is upset or stressed.

A Picture of Calm: Introducing your child to stress-relieving techniques at an early age will teach her skills that can last a lifetime. Visualizations such as "close your eyes and pretend you are on a raft floating in the ocean" can calm your child during challenging situations. You know your child better than anyone, so make your visualization suggestions personalized: "Pretend you are walking slowly on the beach holding Grandpa's hand."

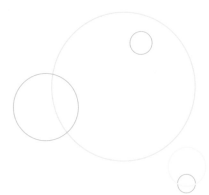

sweet sleep, for baby and you

Getting your baby to sleep and to stay asleep are among the most challenging parenting tasks. There are many opinions about how to approach this issue, including letting your baby cry it out, not letting him cry, putting him down awake or rocking her to sleep. Other choices parents need to consider include co-sleeping or having your child in his own crib or bed. The choices you make will be influenced by your own sleep needs, your child's temperament, and your belief system. Regardless of the way you choose to handle sleep issues, here are some playful parenting tips that will make things easier.

Tips for Making Bedtime Easier

Establish a Bedtime Routine: Children thrive on consistency. Developing a "goodnight" routine for your family makes bedtime easier and less challenging. This may include bath time rituals, story time choices, goodnight kisses for all the stuffed animals in the room, and special music for drifting off to sleep.

Wind Down Before Turning Down: Give your child a "winding down" period where the focus is on soothing, comforting ,and quiet activities. Make sure that you stop active games that can get your child riled up well in advance of bedtime. It's always a wise idea to turn off electronics at least an hour before bedtime because computers, TVs, and video games can sometimes stimulate your child's mind and make it hard to fall asleep.

Down When Drowsy: Rather than rocking or nursing your baby until she is totally asleep, consider laying her down to bed when she is relaxed and drowsy. This will help her get to sleep by herself and therefore fall back asleep if she wakes in the night.

Read a Goodnight Story: Make reading a bedtime story a good habit in your family. Exposing children to this wonderful routine not only soothes them before they go to sleep, but it also helps develop a love of literature.

Take a Deep Breath and Wait: If you hear your baby fuss during the night, don't rush right in. Rather, give him a few minutes to see whether he settles down on his own. Babies may wake several times during the night, and very often they simply go back to sleep on their own.

Keep a Cozy Bed: Never put your child in his crib or bed as a punishment. Young children need to feel that their bed is a special cozy place that isn't associated with discipline.

Back to Sleep: Remember to always put your baby to sleep on her back to decrease the risk of sudden infant death syndrome (SIDS).

Games and Activities to Help Your Child Get to Sleep

Goodnight, Sleep Tight: Create your own goodnight rituals that are special and meaningful for you and your child. Giving him three goodnight kisses, saying "goodnight" to a list of favorite relatives, or reciting your own version of "sleep tight, don't let the bedbugs bite," may be the perfect way to end his day.

Goodnight Songs and Lullabies: Find a special lullaby that you enjoy and sing it to your child each night. With time, this will become a favored part of her goodnight routine that you will both treasure.

Blankies and Huggies »

A favorite soft toy or blanket can help a child feel more secure on her way to sleep. This may become a sacred object that your child truly needs to get herself to sleep, so be extra careful about not losing it and taking it with you on trips. Even if you are clever enough to have more than one blue bunny rabbit, your baby may have a distinct preference for the smell, feel, and appearance of her original one.

Pillow Talk: There is something special about the quiet hush that happens around bedtime. Aside from reading books, tell stories about what you did during the day or about your family or try made-up tales.

Going on a Safari: Hide your child's stuffed animals around her darkened bedroom. Go on a safari together as you use a flashlight to search for her hidden friends. Say a special goodnight to each one.

Winding Down Games: Older preschoolers can use visualizations to help them relax and drift off to sleep. Have your child close his eyes while you tell him to imagine a special, calming scene, such as floating in a balloon, drifitng on a raft, or smelling flowers in a garden.

First This, Then That: Use photos or pictures to create a schedule of goodnight activities, such as putting toys away, getting undressed and into the bath, brushing teeth, and going to bed. You can make it into a fun nightly game by asking, "What comes next?" and having your child check her special picture chart.

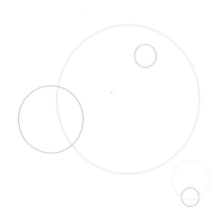

dressing and diapering

Dressing and diapering come up several times every day and young children do not always want to cooperate. Keeping things playful, stress-free, and relaxed can make these routine activities go a little smoother.

Tips for Making Dressing and Diapering Your Baby Easier

Keep It Together: Have everything you need for diapering close at hand with unbreakable mirrors and dangling toys near the changing table to entertain your baby. Keep a variety of small toys in a basket to quickly hand to a child who needs distracting.

Let Your Child Choose: When you ask your child whether she wants to wear the red shirt or the blue shirt, she may focus on happily making her own choice rather than the fact that she didn't want to get dressed at all.

Let Individuality Blossom: Allow your child to develop his own sense of style. As children get older, they have their own opinions and preferences. Wearing cowboy boots with shorts may not be your look, but for your preschooler, it may be exactly what he loves. Most of the time conflicts over what to wear just aren't worth the struggle.

You Are So Beautiful: Hang a full-length, unbreakable mirror in your child's room so he can see how great he looks in his outfit. You can sing a special song and have your child dance in front of the mirror in his special attire. By making mirror time part of your dressing routine, your child will be more cooperative about putting on his clothes.

Games and Activities to Make Diapering and Dressing Playful

Knock Your Socks Off: Once babies develop the dexterity needed to grasp and pull, getting their socks off becomes a fun activity. Put brightly colored socks on their feet and hands and see what happens.

My Dress Is a Mess: Make up silly rhymes when getting your child dressed or use tried-and-true favorites: "This is the way we put on our shoes, put on our shoes, put on our shoes. This is the way we put on our shoes, so early in the morning."

Turn Objections into Giggles: Playful parents understand how to use humor effectively. Instead of a struggle dressing, turn things around and ask silly questions, such as "Do your socks go on your head? Do your shoes go in your ear?"

Suit Up Your Superhero: Instead of just dressing your child in her purple shirt, avoid struggles by putting on her "Super-Duper Superhero" purple shirt. Older toddlers and preschoolers love to pretend and get a charge out of getting superhero powers.

splish, splash, we're taking a bath

Bath time can be one of the most enjoyable, relaxing times of day for you and your child, so slow down and enjoy it. As part of a bedtime ritual it's a great way to help children wind down and get ready for sleep. It can also be a special Daddy time if Mom is doing most of the daytime caregiving. Special toys and games enhance the bath time experience and provide opportunities for learning, sensory exploration, language development, and pretend play.

✛ **Safety Tip: Never leave your child unattended in the bath even for a second.**

Tips for Making Bath Time Enjoyable

Be Prepared: Having all your rubber ducks in a row is a good tactic for bath time. The more organized you are, the easier it is to focus on the task at hand: convincing your child that bath time is both necessary and fun. Get the towel, washcloth, soap, and shampoo ready before your child gets into the tub.

Rubber Ducks Aren't the Only Bath Toy: Be creative with bath toys. Plastic spoons, measuring cups, funnels, and empty shampoo bottles make great bath toys.

Down the Drain: Sometimes it is harder to get your child out of the tub than it is to get him into the bath. One good strategy is to let your child help you flip the drain switch and watch the water disappear and turn the towel into a magic cape just waiting for Superman.

A Hair at a Time: If your child hates getting her hair washed, first practice with water only and then slowly increase the amount of suds you use. Sing a special hair washing song to make it fun and to distract her. Try "splish, splash, I'm taking a bath" or your own chant. Using a plastic visor or having a washcloth on hand to keep the shampoo out of your child's eyes may also do the trick. Keep plastic cups in the bath as a fun way to let your child dump water on her own head and make a game out of what could be a struggle.

Games and Activities for Making Bath Time Fun

Sponge Squeeze: Watching water drip from a sponge is great fun for little ones. Give your child a variety of soft sponges to play with in the bath. Squeezing them will strengthen his hands and help develop those fine motor muscles that are so important for drawing and writing.

Rhyme Time: While you bathe your child, make up simple rhymes that reinforce learning about body parts. "Oh my, I'm washing your eye! Oh dear, I'm washing your ear!" Having fun with your child as you sing songs and make rhymes is a great way to enjoy time together, even during bath time.

Offer a Range of Tubby Toys: Once your child can sit by herself in the tub, she will love playing with a variety of toys. Let her wash her baby dolls and farm animals, provide a variety of containers and funnels for pouring and splashing, poke holes in the bottom of margarine tubs to make a sieve, and give her a spray mist bottle to clean the tub.

Bring Bubbles into the Bath: Using nontoxic bubble solution and a wand, blow bubbles for your child while he's taking a bath. Older children love to take turns and catch the bubbles. Keep the bubbles at water level by getting long plastic tubing from the hardware store and surprising your child by blowing a cascade of bubbles into the tub.

Draw Me a Bath: Crayons specially designed for use in the bathtub can unleash your child's artistic side. Because they are saved for bath time only, they will entice even a resistant child into the tub.

Spoon Some Bath Soup: Create "bath soup" while you wash your child. Have your child stir up a bowl of soup made from bathwater, a bit of shampoo, hair conditioner, or liquid soap.

Catch the Colored Ice Cubes: For a special bath time treat, make colored ice cubes by adding a drop of nontoxic food coloring to the water in each section of an ice cube tray. When put into the tub, they are slippery and fun to catch. Use only a few at a time because when they melt, the water will turn all shades of funky colors.

Have a Whale of a Time: Make your child a whale for the bathtub out of an empty plastic gallon carton or juice jug. Turn the jug on its side so that the handle is on top and draw a mouth shape on the base of the jug. The whale scoop is ready for swimming, scooping, and sinking into the deepest parts of the bathtub. Add small plastic fish for the whale to gobble up.

let's eat

Mealtime is a special family event. It's when family members come together and talk about the events of the day, share feelings, and exchange stories. In today's culture, many families don't preserve the all-important "dinnertime" experience. Too often, separate meals are prepared for each family member, and everyone eats in front of the television or computer. Avoid falling into this habit. Families who regularly share meals have children who do better in school, are less likely to be overweight, have better conversational skills, and connect as a family.

You can establish mealtime as family time from the start with appropriate planning and a degree of tolerance for interruptions and messiness. Eating out as a family in a restaurant will be much easier when the pattern has been established at home.

Tips for Making Mealtime Pleasant

Keep Meals Simple: Every meal does not need to be a gourmet event. Remember, young children prefer simple foods—just keep the choices healthy.

It's on the Yucky List: Let your child have a "don't like" list; everyone is not going to love every kind of food you serve. Allow your child to have a list of three items that she doesn't like. These are the foods she doesn't need to try when they are served. For everything else, taking at least one bite is encouraged.

Let Me Help: Involve your children in the meal preparation. Your child is more likely to eat when he has helped shop for the groceries, contributed to the menu, set the table, and participated in the cooking.

I Can Do It!

As children's fine motor skills develop, they become more adept at eating and other self-help activities. Take a deep breath and allow your preschooler the luxury of extra time to do things by herself. There may be a few more messes as she learns to pour her own juice, but the end result will be well worth your patience and support.

Focus on Family Time: Create some mealtime family rituals. Ask each person at the table to share something special or silly that happened that day or have everyone take turns asking fun questions.

Teaching Manners: Encouraging your child to say "please" and "thank you" and to be respectful of others takes time. The most effective way for your child to learn her manners is by watching you interact with others. Recognize that this is a process that takes time. Keep the mood happy and upbeat.

Games and Activities for Enjoyable Eating

Make Finger Food Part of the Meal: It's about more than just eating. Challenge your baby's small motor skills by providing a variety of finger foods, such as peas and Cheerios, that she can pick up to develop dexterity and a sense of accomplishment.

Toy Drop: To keep your baby busy while you are preparing his meals, try tying toys to his high chair with short colorful ribbons. See whether he can discover how to let them drop and then pull them up again. This is a great problem-solving activity for an older infant.

Make It a Taco Night: What could be more fun than building your own taco? Put out all the ingredients in small bowls and let your child pile his favorites into the taco shell. Delicious! Make special recipe nights a weekly event, such as make-your-own pizza or pasta nights.

preparing your child for a new sibling

This can be the happiest of times, but as your family expands everyone has to make adjustments. As exciting as the prospect of becoming a big sister or brother can be, the reality of sharing Mom and Dad, waiting because a newborn baby's needs come first, and suddenly hearing a lot more "no's" can be disconcerting. Preparing your child carefully for her new role and being sensitive to her feelings when her new sibling arrives can make things a bit easier and happier for everyone.

Tips for Preparing Your Child to Be a Big Brother or Sister

Chitchat: Encourage your child to "talk" to your baby in the womb, tell stories, and sing songs. Let him know what an important and special teacher he'll be for the new baby.

Practice Being a Big Sister: As the big day nears, help your child practice for her new role by bathing her baby dolls, pushing her dolls in a doll stroller, and reading books about babies to her dolls.

Getting Ready: Let your child help you prepare the baby's room, sort out baby clothes, and decide which of his things he will share with the new baby. As he helps you with these chores, he will feel empowered and grown-up.

Take a Tour: If your hospital has sibling tours, take advantage of this opportunity. Your child will feel better knowing where you will be and what to expect.

Welcome Home

Prepare the art supplies well in advance of your hospital stay so that your child and her caregiver can make a special welcome home sign to proudly hang on the door for you and the new baby. You can also make an "I'm the Big Sister" sign for your child to decorate and hang proudly on her door.

Prepare Your Child for Your Absence: This may be the first time your child has spent a night away from you. Be honest and matter-of-fact. "I will be sleeping in the hospital for two nights, and then I will be bringing our new baby home." Practice talking with her on the telephone so that she is ready to hear your voice when you call from the hospital. Talk about where she will be staying and who will be watching her in your absence.

My Baby Looks Beautiful: Let your child pick out a special outfit for the new baby to wear when he comes home. This is one of many choices you can give your older child, because there will be countless changes in his life with the arrival of a new baby in the family.

It's from My Baby: Walking through the door with the new baby is even more exciting when she "brings" a gift to her big brother. A stuffed animal or that special toy he's been wanting will be treasured even more when it is from his new baby sister.

Games and Activities for the New Big Brother or Sister

Where Will the Baby Sleep?: Be silly with your child. Will the new baby sleep in a garbage can, in a rocking chair? Humor can diffuse anxiety and resentment.

My Baby's Special Picture: Your older child will love making a special sign with his new baby's name. Let him draw and decorate a small piece of cardboard for his new sibling and proudly hang it on the outside of baby's crib or cradle.

Quiet Time: Make a "Shhhh . . . baby sleeping" sign with your child to hang on the door of the baby's room when he's sleeping. Having your older child in charge of keeping the house quiet will give her a sense of control and will help avoid power struggles.

I'm a "Big Brother": With your child, create a special book of things that your big boy is doing to prepare for the new baby and then add photos after the baby's arrival. Let him tell you what the captions should be. Don't edit out the negative comments; remember, it's his book, and these are his feelings about having a new family member.

Read to Me!: There are many wonderful books to help prepare your child for the role of big brother or big sister. Spend lots of time cuddling together and reading while giving your child the opportunity to talk about his or her feelings.

places to go and people to meet

Running errands or waiting for appointments doesn't have to be tedious and boring. Something as simple as driving to the grocery store can open new worlds for your child as you sing songs, point out sights, or talk about your day. Just as you search for a magazine or take out an electronic gadget to help pass the time, your child also needs interesting stimulation when in the car, on a plane, at the doctor's office, or at the supermarket.

When you are in the midst of a crisis, you might use deep breathing, meditation, a chat with a friend, or other calming techniques. Your child feels the same way and depends on you to offer support. Children find relief and connection through playful exchanges. Playful parents come prepared with ideas, toys, books, and "dinosaur voices" to help pass the time and defuse what might become a meltdown.

Preparing an "On the Go Kit"

Whether it is visiting Grandma, waiting for your dinner in a restaurant, or traveling on a plane, there will be many times that you and your child are simply sitting and waiting. Be prepared to make the most of these experiences by keeping an "On the Go Kit" handy. Change the items in the kit regularly to keep it novel so that there is always something new and exciting to engage your child during long waits and tedious times.

Use your imagination and include things you know are of interest to your child. Some suggested items to get you started are in the sidebar.

why outside play is important

In this era of television, video games, computers, and urban sprawl, our children are spending less and less time outdoors. Many are nature deprived, having limited opportunities to experience the mountains, play on the beach, or just walk in a field of green grass.

Fitness begins in the early years. Encourage a love of nature by taking your child to the park or out on walks on a regular basis. Set the stage for a healthy lifestyle by regularly enjoying the outdoors and exercising with your child. Create backyard play spaces that are safe and inviting. Spend time breathing the fresh air and smelling the flowers. Garden together and be amazed as your new flowers spring to life.

Tips for Making Outdoor Playtime Fun and Interesting

Walk in the Rain: What may seem like inclement weather for you is actually a delight for your child. It's fun to walk in the rain with an umbrella, and boots are perfect for puddle jumping and splashing. Unleash your inner child and enjoy this special time together.

Dig Some Playground Games: When you go to the playground with your child, bring along extra shovels and pails to share. Blowing bubbles is a great way to entertain a group of children and help your child meet new friends.

Games and Activities for Enjoyable Outdoor Playtime

Play Sponge Tag: This is a silly outdoor game that will keep the whole family laughing. Get several sponges and put them into a bucket of water. Choose one person to be "it." This person throws the sponges at the other players until someone is "tagged."

Dig for Sand Treasures: Make treasure nuggets by letting your children paint clean rocks with their favorite color paint. Hide them in the sandbox for your gold diggers to discover.

Make a Tree Rubbing: On your next walk, bring home a bit of nature. Find a tree with rough bark and tape or hold over it a piece of construction paper. Use the side of an unwrapped crayon to make an interesting texture rub.

Use Your Green Thumb: Bulbs sprout fairly quickly. Plant some in a glass container so your child can observe the growth of both the roots and the stems. Transfer the rooted bulbs to your garden and watch them grow. If you have a garden, involve your child in planting, watering, and caring for it. Plants that grow quickly from seed like sunflowers are especially reinforcing for young gardeners.

Take a Nature Walk: There is so much to explore. Walk slowly, pause frequently, and bring along a pail to collect beautiful leaves, rocks, sticks, and flowers. This is a great time to encourage your child to use all five senses. Notice the way the air smells after the rain, listen for the crickets chirping in the early morning, and watch for the stars as they fully emerge in the evening sky.

The Benefit of Backyard Spaces

Create a safe space for your child to play outdoors. Consider sandboxes, playhouses, climbing structures, swing sets, and a hard surface for riding toys. An outdoor art studio is easy to create—all you need is a table or an easel. If you don't have a yard, get creative on your porch or patio.

Water, Water, Everywhere: On a warm day there is no better place to be than in a wading pool. Keep in mind the basic health and safety rules. Never leave a child alone in or near any type of water. Make sure the water is clean and free of algae and mold, so dump and replace it often.

✚ **Safety Tip: Always dump the water out at the end of playtime.**

Release Your Creative Side: Children love the freedom of painting outdoors. A bucket of water and a paintbrush can keep a toddler busy for a long time. Writing on the sidewalk with chalk, wet or dry, makes for unusual and special drawings.

Giddy-Up, Horsey: Ride-on toys are great for imaginative play, and there are many different types from which to choose. Ride-on vehicles facilitate early motor development as well as enhance imaginative play skills. Fire trucks, ride-on animals, grocery carts, and ride-in coupes and police cars have great appeal and lasting play value. Wagons are wonderful for hauling special items and taking a friend for a ride. Ride-on vehicles are a particularly good investment because they are great for early walkers and are still fun for your preschooler to pretend with.

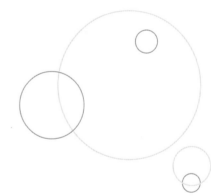

Slimy, Squirmy fun: Young children are totally intrigued by bugs, tadpoles, and lizards. Get a special bug box and bring some home. Take good care of your creatures and teach responsibility and respect for all living things.

Go to Places Real and Imagined: Running and playing outdoors naturally encourages a variety of dramatic play themes. Shopping, "driving" to Disney World, playing pirates, and having a restaurant can all happen outside with a variety of props and a little encouragement. There are infinite possibilities when it comes to outdoor pretend play, so bring out the buckets, ride-on vehicles, dress-up clothes, and paper and crayons and let your child's imagination soar.

eating out

Sharing a meal in a restaurant with your child can be a pleasant experience if you make good choices and plan ahead. While it may not exactly be a fine dining experience, eating out as a family can be fun. It's always helpful to go to restaurants that encourage families and where you won't feel uncomfortable when your toddler spills his sippy cup or throws crackers on the floor.

Tips for Making Dining Out Easy and Fun

Focus on Me!: Know that you will have to pay attention to your child. This is not the time for an in-depth discussion with your spouse about your mortgage or future plans.

Families Are Welcome: Choose child-friendly restaurants where there is something on the menu your child will eat. Look for a restaurant that has high chairs and if necessary, call ahead to find out about seating arrangements. Will your child be able to stay in a stroller or baby carrier if he falls asleep?

I'm Hungry!: When you are dining out with children, time is of the essence. Order appetizers as soon as you are seated or bring along finger foods to keep a hungry child from having to wait too long to eat. A tired, hungry, cranky child is no fun in a restaurant. Try to dine at the time your child is not overtired or extremely hungry. Ask for the check as soon as the last course is served. Also, try to avoid the lunch and dinner rush hours so that you won't have to wait and you can get served quickly.

Games and Activities to Keep Your Child Entertained While Dining Out

Ice, Ice Baby: Babies can be entertained with ice on their high chair tray, especially when you participate in the fun. A cold wet ice cube is a great way for your little one to learn fine motor control as she tries to pick it up. Using words like "cold," "freezing," and "wet" also support language development as your child enjoys this frozen fun.

Tear It Up: Paper napkins can be drawn on or ripped into shreds. These simple activities can entertain your child until the food is served. Fold the wrapping of a straw into small pieces and drop droplets of water or juice on it and see what happens. Put several "to go" lids through a straw to make an interesting temporary toy.

Tell Me a Story: Transform the silverware into talking "puppets" and introduce your child to Mr. Spoon and Mrs. Fork. Make up silly songs and stories as they talk to each other.

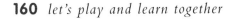

shopping and strolling

It is a big wide world out there with a lot to be explored and learned. Shopping and strolling with your child can become an adventure. When you are rushed or stressed and focused only on getting your chores done it is difficult to take advantage of the educational opportunities that abound. So choose an opportunity when you have ample time and your child is both well rested and fed.

Tips for Making Shopping and Strolling Easy and Fun

Yummy Treats: Keeping a stash of non-messy, no-spill snacks on hand during your outing will fend off a hunger attack. Interesting, child-friendly containers make self-feeding fun and help keep your child entertained.

Keep Toys Close at Hand: Attaching your child's special toys to her stroller will help prevent losing these precious items. Plastic links work particularly well. Always remember to keep strings short to avoid a safety hazard.

Consider Stroller Choices: There are many good options for strollers. Think about the ways you are going to use your purchase. If you live in a city or enjoy taking long walks, consider a sturdy stroller that has a reclining seat and storage space underneath. For short trips to the store, lightweight folding strollers are usually sufficient.

Let Me Help!

While grocery shopping, involve your little one in your selections; for example, let him count out four oranges and put them into the bag. Talk about the colors and shapes of the packages. Hunt together for your child's favorite cereal, letting him spot the special logo that tells you it's the right one. Have your child help you find what you need: "Can you get me a bigger can of beans?" Talk about all the different kinds of pastas you see on the shelf. Let your child choose something new to try for dinner.

Games and Activities to Make Shopping and Strolling Interesting and Fun

It's on the List: Make a list for your shopping venture and let your child be the list keeper to help you check off your purchases or errands. Even children who can't yet read learn important lessons about the value of the printed word when they watch you refer to the list. For a special treat, cut and paste or download pictures of the items and have your chld find them.

Talk to Me: When you have your baby in a shopping cart, make sure you talk with him as you go. Babies and toddlers stay calm and entertained when you chat with them and sing songs while shopping.

Experience New Sensations: The sights, sounds, and smells of the store provide wonderful learning opportunities. Sensory experiences are all over the store—smelling the produce, feeling the cold milk container, touching the shiny pots, or listening for the hum of the freezers. Talk with your child as you go through the store. "Do you like the smell of bread baking?" "Feel the bumpy cantaloupe!"

Check Me Out: When you are waiting in the checkout line at the grocery store, play simple games to keep your child entertained. Count the items on the grocery belt. Play "I spy" something red. Wonder together whether it will be raining when you get outside.

Chips Ahoy: If your baby is getting antsy in the supermarket, hand her a small, sealed bag of chips. The bag makes great noises as you crinkle and crush it, creating a great diversion. It is a small price to pay for a temporary new toy.

planes, trains, and auto- mobiles

Traveling with children takes planning and organization. There are times when CDs and DVDs can be lifesavers, but there are so many great opportunities for play and learning when traveling. Talk with your child about the sights and sounds you see out the window. Introduce new vocabulary, wonder together how things work, and talk about where everyone is going and what you are going to see around the next corner. These opportunities give you focused attention time for you and your child, particularly when you drive without distractions, such as the cell phone.

Tips for Making Traveling Stress-Free

Fly Me to the Moon: Taking a trip on an airplane is a longer process than just flying time. Check-in, security lines, and luggage waits can be longer than the actual flight, so you need to be well prepared. Being organized is vital so that you can easily access favorite toys, snacks, bottles, and books. During the flight, take advantage of the times that the seat belt sign is off to take your child for a walk. For long flights, bring a small pillow and child-size blankets to encourage naps or bedtime. Everyone has the tendency to overpack, but packing simply and lightly is often the best way to go.

Keep Your Eyes on the Road!: Even short trips can take a toll on parents and children alike. You always have to pay attention to the road, even with a crying toddler in tow. Unless it's an emergency, the best strategy is to just ignore the tears until you can safely pull over.

Toys on the Go

The best strategy for car travel is to be prepared with a variety of age-appropriate toys and books to keep your child occupied. To avoid, "Daddy, I dropped my puppy," choose toys that can be attached to the car seat with short plastic links. On long trips, at rest stops, rotate the toys to keep things novel. Infants are intrigued by childproof mirrors, toddlers enjoy chunky books, and preschoolers love bringing their little people along for rides.

Games and Activities to Make Traveling Fun and Easy

From Mozart to Rock: Keep an interesting supply of music CDs in your car or load them onto your iPod. Use this time to expose your baby, toddler, or preschooler to a wide variety of music genres.

Tell Me a Story: The intimate space of a car or plane is the perfect environment to tell stories. Even the youngest baby loves the sound of your voice, and although she isn't following the story line, you are teaching her to enjoy storytelling. Older children can take turns with you telling their own special stories.

Can You Find the Letters of Your Name?: Have your preschooler look in sequence for the letters in his name on signs, billboards, and license plates. Once he has found the completed spelling of his name it's your turn to play.

Alphabet Sightings: Go through the alphabet looking for things starting with each letter: "Who can find something that starts with the letter *B* first?"

Red Light, Green Light: A fun way to teach colors is to bring your child's attention to the stoplight. It's also fun to count the seconds until the light changes.

Logo Hunt: A first step toward reading is recognizing that a symbol has meaning. Point out the logos for your favorite stores and restaurants. Before you know it, your child will be able to spot them before you do.

shots, Band-Aids, and medicine . . . oh my!

Doctors' visits can be overwhelming for some young children and stressful for you. Medical procedures, especially ones that are scary, like getting shots or taking blood, can be especially difficult. Hospital stays can be made easier with clever planning and a sense of playful nurturance.

Tips for Making Doctors' Visits Less Stressful

Make Waiting Fun: Waiting for your doctor's appointment is a time when anxiety builds for both you and your child. It is often hard to focus on entertaining or distracting your little one; however, it does make a big difference. Bring your "On the Go Kit" and stay focused on your child's needs. Your child will appreciate your attention and become less stressed in anticipation of his visit with the doctor.

Stay Close: Your child looks to you for comfort and protection, and this is often intensified when at the doctor's office. Naturally, your child's favorite place will be in your arms, but when that is not possible, holding her hand or rubbing her back will also help. Sometimes the medical team will discourage you from remaining with your child, but remember that you know your child best, and it is okay to insist on staying.

Find Ways to Distract Your Child: Sometimes the best thing you can do is provide a distraction while your child is in an uncomfortable position or is undergoing a painful procedure. With babies, rocking, patting, singing, giving a pacifier, or shaking a rattle can be helpful. Toddlers can be distracted with bubbles, light-up toys, music, and pop-up books. Silly games can be helpful with preschoolers. Try counting, making a pinwheel turn, blowing bubbles, or telling silly stories.

It's Okay to Cry: Let your child know that it is okay to cry and to be scared. At the same time, emphasize the importance of cooperating with the doctor. "I know you're scared, and it's okay to cry, but I need you to stay very, very still."

Whenever Possible, Give Choices: "Which arm do you want to get the shot?" "Who should hold you, Mommy or Daddy?" "Which Band-Aid do you choose?" Providing choices is a great distraction and helps your child feel more in control.

Make a List and Check It Twice: Have your questions ready because it's easy in the heat of the moment to forget everything you intended to ask your physician.

Modulate Your Emotions: Your child is watching you. Your anxiety and fear are contagious. Remember that you are your child's most influential and important teacher. By modeling appropriate emotional responses to stress and anxiety, you are teaching your child to do the same.

Watch Your Words: Remember when you are speaking with the medical team that your child will be listening. Be sensitive to his feelings and lack of control during these times. Be careful about not overdramatizing your child's symptoms. Telling the doctor that Jonathan gets a stomachache every morning to avoid going to school is a sure way for that behavior to continue. Likewise, if you have true concerns about your child's symptoms, be careful not to frighten her because she may be listening intently to everything you say. Consider having a family member or friend watch your child in the waiting room if you are planning on having a serious discussion with the doctor.

Be Honest with Your Child

It's best to tell a child what to expect. Being truthful builds trust and confidence. Many parents may be afraid that if they tell their child ahead of time about scary events they will have a tantrum. Yes, they might, but it is far better to build trust, and in the long run your child will feel more secure knowing what to expect. Keep your explanations matter-of-fact and watch for your child's reactions so you can modulate how much to share.

Facing the Scary Stuff

There are some aspects of visiting the doctor that are just plain scary. Of course, children cannot play with or touch needles, but they can play with tongue depressors, cotton balls, and Band-Aids. These real objects help diffuse the anxiety associated with them. You can incorporate them into your child's doctor kit or include them with other art materials to make art collages with glue, glitter, paint, and tape on cardboard.

Games and Activities to Help Your Child Cope with Doctors' Visits

Playing Doctor to Address Fears: Playing out doctors' visits or medical procedures at home helps your child understand what will happen and provides her with a sense of control. Playing doctor, rather than patient, puts your child in the driver's seat and helps her feel more powerful. You can pretend to be scared and let your child reassure you that everything will be okay. You can also be an uncooperative patient, playfully refusing to take your medicine and then letting your child coerce you into opening your mouth.

Dolly's Boo-Boos: Once your child is old enough to enjoy pretend play with his dolls, little people, and stuffed animals, get him a children's doctor kit to help take away their boo-boos. Not only will playing with the kit help during the times he is ill, but it will also be a way to desensitize him to the scary aspects of going to the doctor.

Picture This: Drawing pictures about their experiences helps children cope with scary feelings. It is also helpful to let your child talk about her picture to further process her emotions.

My Trip to the Doctor: Reading books with your child creates closeness and offers a world of new information. Creating your own storybooks is a more personal way to describe events in her life. Take photographs of your child's visit to the doctor or hospital, documenting every part of her experience. Paste or tape the photos onto heavy paper and write words underneath to describe each picture. For older children, take dictation and scribe their own words. Staple the pages together and create a real book written by you and your child.

tried and true
Classic Songs and Rhymes for
Babies, Toddlers, and Preschoolers

Having a repertoire of songs that you share with your child is a wonderful way to enhance language, fine-tune listening skills, teach specific concepts, and enjoy special time together. You will find that there are times when familiar songs are great for soothing a grumpy child, getting through a long car ride, changing a mood with laughter, or distracting a child in the midst of a difficult medical procedure.

The following songs are traditional favorites and there are countless other ones for you to choose. Find your favorite, cherished songs from your own childhood to introduce to your child.

"Pop Goes the Weasel"

All around the cobbler's bench,
The monkey chased the weasel;
The monkey thought it was all fun,
Pop! goes the weasel.

A penny for a spool of thread,
A penny for a needle;
That's the way the money goes,
 Pop! goes the weasel.

Up and down the city road,
In and out of the Eagle;
That's the way the money goes,
Pop! goes the weasel.

"This Little Piggy"

This little piggy went to market,
This little piggy stayed home,
This little piggy had roast beef,
This little piggy had none,
And this little piggy went wee, wee, wee,
all the way home.
(Do this as you wiggle each toe on one of your child's feet, starting with the largest one and ending with a tickling run of your fingers over her body.)

"London Bridge Is Falling Down"

London Bridge is falling down,
Falling down, falling down,
London Bridge is falling down,
My fair lady.

Build it up with wood and clay,
Wood and clay, wood and clay,
Build it up with wood and clay,
My fair lady.

"Baa, Baa, Black Sheep"

Baa, baa, black sheep,
Have you any wool?
Yes, sir, yes, sir,
Three bags full;
One for my master,
And one for my dame,
And one for the little boy
Who lives down the lane.

"Oh, Where, Oh, Where Has My Little Dog Gone?"

Oh, where, oh, where has my little dog gone?
Oh, where, oh, where can he be?
With his ears so short and his tail so long,
Oh, where, oh, where can he be?

"The Eensy Weensy Spider"

The eensy weensy spider
Climbed up the waterspout;
Down came the rain
And washed the spider out;
Out came the sun
And dried up all the rain;
And the eensy weensy spider
Climbed up the spout again.

"Hey Diddle Diddle"

Hey diddle diddle,
The cat and the fiddle,
The cow jumped over the moon;
The little dog laughed
To see such fun,
And the dish ran away with the spoon.

"It's Raining, It's Pouring"

It's raining, it's pouring;
The old man is snoring.
He bumped his head
And went to bed
And couldn't get up in the morning.

"Ants Go Marching"

The ants go marching one by one, hurrah, hurrah
The ants go marching one by one, hurrah, hurrah
The ants go marching one by one,
The little one stops to suck his thumb
And they all go marching down to the ground
To get out of the rain, BOOM! BOOM! BOOM!

The ants go marching two by two, hurrah, hurrah
The ants go marching two by two, hurrah, hurrah
The ants go marching two by two,
The little one stops to tie his shoe
And they all go marching down to the ground
To get out of the rain, BOOM! BOOM! BOOM!

The ants go marching three by three, hurrah, hurrah
The ants go marching three by three, hurrah, hurrah
The ants go marching three by three,
The little one stops to climb a tree
And they all go marching down to the ground
To get out of the rain, BOOM! BOOM! BOOM!

"You Are My Sunshine"

You are my sunshine,
My only sunshine
You make me happy
When skies are gray.
You'll never know, dear,
How much I love you,
Please don't take my sunshine away.

"One, Two, Buckle My Shoe"

One, two, buckle my shoe;
Three, four, shut the door;
Five, six, pick up sticks;
Seven, eight, lay them straight;
Nine, ten, a big fat hen;
Lays her eggs for gentlemen.

"Pat-a Cake"

Pat-a-cake, pat-a-cake, baker's man,
Bake me a cake as fast as you can,
Roll it and knead it and mark it with a B,
And put it in the oven for Baby and Me!

"Mr. Sun"

Oh, Mr. Sun, Sun, Mr. Golden Sun,
Please shine down on me.
Oh, Mr. Sun, Sun, Mr. Golden Sun,
Hiding behind a tree.
These little children are asking you
To please come out so we can play with you
Oh, Mr. Sun, Sun, Mr. Golden Sun,
Please shine down on me.

Oh, Mr. Sun, Sun, Mr. Golden Sun,
Please shine down on me.
Oh, Mr. Sun, Sun, Mr. Golden Sun,
Hiding behind a tree.
These little children are asking you
To please come out so we can play with you.
Oh, Mr. Sun, Sun, Mr. Golden Sun,
Please shine down on, please shine down on,
Please shine down on me.

"Rain, Rain, Go Away"

Rain, rain, go away,
Come again another day,
Little Kenneth wants to play.

"Do Your Ears Hang Low?"

Do your ears hang low?
Do they wobble to and fro?
Can you tie them in a knot?
Can you tie them in a bow?
Can you throw them o'er your shoulder
Like a Continental Soldier?
Do your ears hang low?

Do your ears hang high?
Do they reach up to the sky?
Do they wrinkle when they're wet?
Do they straighten when they're dry?
Can you wave them at your neighbor
With an element of flavor?
Do your ears hang high?

Do your ears hang wide?
Do they flap from side to side?
Do they wave in the breeze
From the slightest little sneeze?
Can you soar above the nation
With a feeling of elevation?
Do your ears hang wide?

"Hokey Pokey"

This perennial favorite is a great way to get your child moving and develop body awareness.

You put your right hand in,
You take your right hand out,
You put your right hand in and you
shake it all about,
You do the hokey pokey and you
turn yourself around,
That's what it's all about!

(Continue with other body parts: left hand, right leg, hand, elbow, neck, whole self, and so on)

"Three Little Ducks"

Three little ducks that I once knew
Fat ones, skinny ones, red ones, too.
But the one little duck with the feather on his back,
He ruled the others with a quack, quack, quack.
Down to the river they all would go,
Wiggle, waggle, wiggle, waggle to and fro.
But the one little duck with the feather on his back,
He ruled the others with a quack, quack, quack.
He ruled the others with a quack, quack, quack.

"Row, Row, Row Your Boat"

Row, row, row your boat
Gently down the stream,
Merrily, merrily, merrily, merrily,
Life is but a dream.
(Varying your pace makes this song even more fun.)

"Head, Shoulders, Knees and Toes"

Head, shoulders, knees and toes, knees and toes
Head, shoulders, knees and toes, knees and toes
Eyes and ears and mouth and nose
Head, shoulders knees and toes,
Knees and toes!
(Place both hands on each body part as they are mentioned. Speed up with each verse!

"The Wheels on the Bus"

The wheels on the bus go round and round,
round and round, round and round,
The wheels on the bus go round and round,
all through the town.

The people on the bus go up and down,
up and down, up and down,
The people on the bus go up and down,
all through the town.

(Repeat with verses below.)

The horn on the bus goes beep, beep, beep
The wipers on the bus go swish, swish, swish
The money on the bus goes jingle, jingle, jingle
The babies on the bus go wah, wah, wah
The mommies on the bus say shh, shh, shh
The daddies on the bus say "I love you, I love you,
I love you"
The kitties on the bus say meow, meow, meow

*(Add hand movements, for each verse: roll your
fists around one another, honk a horn, swish your
hands, and so on)*

"Jack and Jill"

Jack and Jill went up the hill to fetch a pail of water
Jack fell down and broke his crown
And Jill came tumbling after.

"Old MacDonald"

Old MacDonald had a farm, e-i-e-i-o.
And on his farm he had a cow, e-i-e-i-o.
With a moo, moo here and a moo, moo there,
Here a moo, there a moo, everywhere a moo, moo,
Old MacDonald had a farm, e-i e-i-o.
*(Repeat with various farm animals and their
sounds.)*

"If You're Happy and You Know It"

If you're happy and you know it, clap your hands,
If you're happy and you know it, clap your hands,
If you're happy and you know it, then your face will
surely show it,
If you're happy and you know it, clap your hands.

*(Try the song inserting different emotions or add
different movements, such as touch your nose,
swing your arms, jump three times, and turn
around.)*

If you're sad and you know it, dry your tears.
If you're mad and you know it, stamp your feet.
If you're surprised and you know it, say "oh my."

Acknowledgments

We have had the pleasure of listening to the laughter and watching the joy exuded from thousands of children and their parents as they played together at our program at the Mailman Segal Center of Nova Southeastern University in Florida. It was through our professional work there that we learned about the importance of play and the unique opportunity for building and strengthening relationships that these experiences nurture in families. Dr. Marilyn "Mickey" Segal, our mentor, paved the way by showing us how to gracefully and thoughtfully encourage even the youngest infant into playful interactions. Her wisdom guided not only our professional paths but also the work of countless others in the field of early childhood development. The world is a happier place because of her.

Heartfelt appreciation for the encouragement and direction provided by Philip Klein, our attorney extraordinaire. He spent countless hours supporting us and helped make this book a reality. A special acknowledgement goes to Rebecca Salgado, who diligently typed and edited our zillion track changes and handwritten scribbles and never lost her smile throughout.

We deeply thank all those families who allowed us to enter into their special world as they played and learned together. The work we do is an honor.

About the Authors

Dr. Roni Cohen Leiderman and Dr. Wendy Masi specialize in developmental psychology, early childhood development, parenting, and special education. They have been friends and colleagues for more than thirty years and together developed innovative programs for families and children at the Mailman Segal Center for Human Development at Nova Southeastern University in Florida. They have co-authored numerous books on play and child development, been interviewed and featured on national and local television programs and video productions, consulted for toy manufacturers and curriculum developers, and lectured internationally on subjects related to families, autism, and early care and education. Dr. Masi is the mother of four children. Dr. Cohen Leiderman is the mother of two children and has two playful grandchildren.